WE ARE YOUR LEAFS

WE ARE YOUR

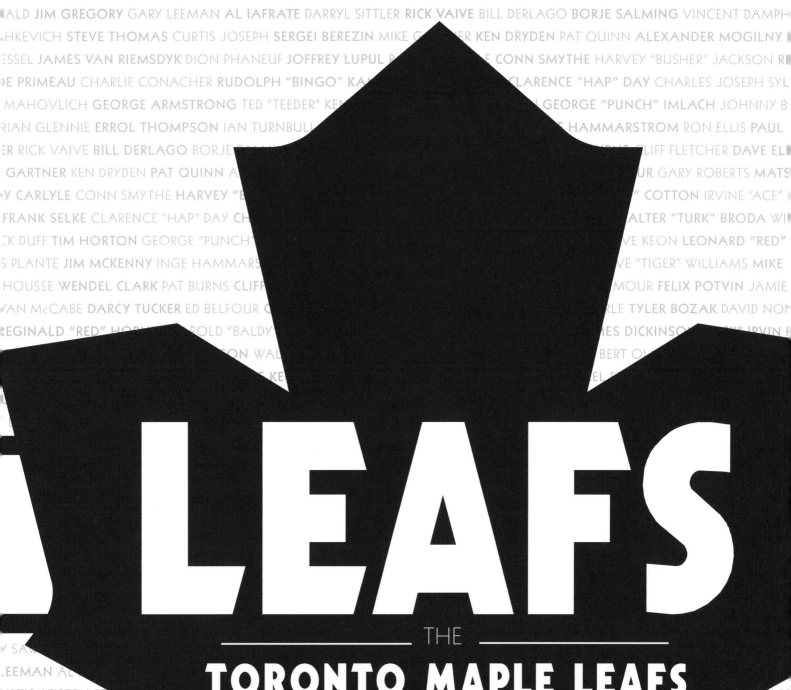

LEAFS

THE

TORONTO MAPLE LEAFS

BOOK OF GREATS

MIKE ULMER

FENN
M&S

Library and Archives Canada Cataloguing in Publication data available upon request.

Published simultaneously in the United States of America by McClelland & Stewart, a division of Random House of Canada Limited P.O. Box 1030, Plattsburgh, New York 12901

Library of Congress Control Number: 2014944362

Edited by Elizabeth Kribs

Typeset in Avenir by M&S, Toronto
Printed and bound in the United States

FENN / McClelland & Stewart,
a division of Random House of Canada Limited
www.randomhouse.ca

1   2   3   4   5   18   17   16   15   14

From left: Frank Mahovlich, Al Arbour, and Bob Pulford

CONTENTS

LEGEND: C = CAPTAIN • 🏒 = HOCKEY HALL OF FAME MEMBER • 🏆 = STANLEY CUP WINNER

RUSSELL CRAWFORD
LEFT WING.

HARRY MEEKING
CENTRE.

KENNETH RANDALL
RIGHT DEFENCE.

CORBETT DENNENY
CENTRE.

HARRY CAMERON
RIGHT DEFENCE.

THE ARENA HOCKEY CLUB OF TORONTO

·1918·

·1919·

RICHARD CARROLL
COACH.

JACK ADAMS
RIGHT WING.

MR. CHARLES QUERRIE
MANAGER.

ALFRED SKINNER
RIGHT WING.

FRANK CARROLL
TRAINER.

CHAMPIONS OF THE WORLD

THE O'BRIEN CUP.

HARRY MUMMERY
LEFT DEFENCE.

HARRY HOLMES
GOAL.

REGINALD NOBLE
CENTRE.

THE STANLEY CUP.

INTRODUCTION

Our story starts about 100 years ago with a Stanley Cup win. Originally, the club was a temporary franchise operated by the Toronto Arena Company, the firm that owned the club's home rink, the Arena Gardens. The existence of the Toronto team was a victory of pragmatism: the NHL had only three other teams, and some concessions had to be made for the burgeoning Toronto hockey market in what would be the first season of the league. The press called them the Blueshirts, or simply the Torontos.

The Arenas – also known as the Blueshirts – captured the 1918 Stanley Cup by defeating the Pacific Coast Hockey Association representatives, the Vancouver Millionaires, in five games. Because the series brought together teams from different leagues, an accommodation had to be made. The Pacific Coast league did not allow forward passing and played with seven players a side; the NHL permitted forward passing and played with six. And so for the best-of-five series, the rules alternated each game. Perhaps not surprisingly, each team won playing under their own rules, which set up a final game that was played under NHL rules. The Blueshirts final win of 2–1 earned a championship for Dick Carroll, a rookie coach who had been elevated from trainer a few months before the final. That victory was inscribed on the Cup 30 years later, cementing in history the successful inaugural season for the Toronto team.

From these modest beginnings, an allegiance has been forged. The Toronto Maple Leafs, whose trials and triumphs were delivered first via radio airwaves to kitchens and living rooms coast to coast, has given the hockey world some of its biggest names – Apps, Kennedy, Bower, Salming, Sittler, Gilmour, Clark, Sundin – Hall of Famers all of them. Thirteen Stanley Cups later, it has established itself as the most popular hockey team on the planet. Leafs Nation is now a borderless state that spans the globe, and the unflagging support of Leafs fans has no equal.

Within these pages are stories that come from a history rich in extraordinary players, exceptional coaches, and team builders. Their stories are pieces of a mosaic written in blue and white, victory and defeat, heartbreak and magnificent success.

MIKE ULMER

THE 1920s

CONN SMYTHE

HARVEY "BUSHER" JACKSON

REGINALD "RED" HORNER

HAROLD "BALDY" COTTON

IRVINE "ACE" BAILEY

FOSTER HEWITT

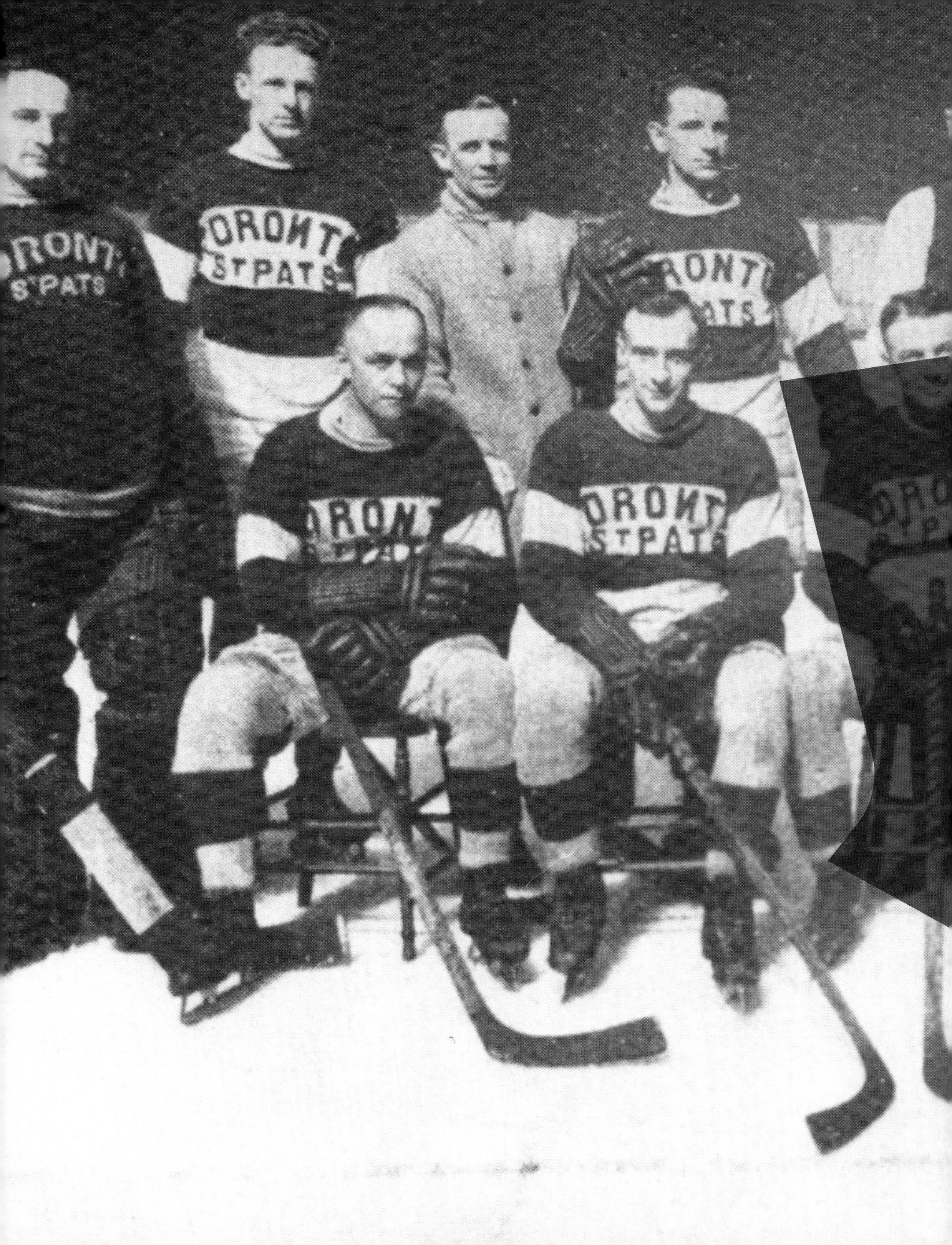

ORONT
ST PATS

TEAM OF THE DECADE
1921–22 TORONTO ST. PATS

REGULAR SEASON RECORD: 13-10-1
PLAYOFF RECORD: 4-2-1

The Leafs' predecessor, the Toronto St. Pats, garnered the city's first Stanley Cup thanks to a star who set a post-season scoring standard for the ages. Cecil Henry "Babe" Dye was the hero of the 1922 Stanley Cup. Dye scored 9 of the St. Pats' 16 goals in the final over Vancouver, including 4 in the fifth and deciding game. His record 9 goals in that 1922 final has never been bettered.

Dye's 38 goals, struck in 29 games in the 1924–25 season, stood as the high-water mark for a Toronto player for 35 years until Frank Mahovlich scored 48 times in the 1960–61 season. Babe Dye led the league in goalscoring three times and was the NHL's top pointgetter in 1923 and 1925. No Leaf has won the scoring title since it was formalized into the Art Ross Trophy in 1948.

After losing two of the first three games, the St. Pats outscored Vancouver 11–1 over the final two contests to breeze to the city's second Stanley Cup.

Princess Elizabeth with Conn Smythe, 1951

CONN SMYTHE

GENERAL MANAGER • 1927–57
COACH • 1927–31

Born: **February 1, 1895, Toronto, Ontario** Died: **November 18, 1980 (85), Toronto, Ontario**
Games: **1,665** Record: **744 W, 612 L, 274 T** Pts. %: **.547**
Stanley Cups: **1932, 1942, 1945, 1947, 1948, 1949, 1951**
Inducted into Hockey Hall of Fame: **1958 (Builder)**

The Toronto Maple Leafs are the product of one man's dream, a man who emerged from poverty to forge an institution on instinct, courage, and ambition. Conn Smythe was born into a poor Toronto family. While studying at the University of Toronto, young Conn was a bantamweight and played for the school hockey team.

Smythe fought in both World Wars. Though just five-foot-seven, he made a natural military man with his tenaciousness and single-minded determination. He won the Military Cross in 1916. After he was shot down and captured in an airborne mission, he made two aborted escape attempts and finished the war as a POW. He would be injured by shrapnel in the Second World War after cajoling his way into combat along with a regiment of athletes and writers he assembled. Smythe felt a kinship with fighting men. "Of a hundred men in the army, you could trust ninety-five of them," he once said. "From a hundred people in civilian life, you're lucky if you can trust five."

His experiences after he returned from the First World War would justify that view. In 1926, when Colonel John Hammond was assembling players for his new team, the New York Rangers, he tapped Smythe because of his wide contacts in the university, amateur, and senior player ranks. Smythe did an excellent job; his hand-picked roster would win the Stanley Cup two years later, but last-minute politicking induced Hammond to fire Smythe in favour of the more-tested Lester Patrick.

The dismissal only stoked Smythe's interest in fielding a team of his own, and when word reached him that the Toronto St. Pats were losing money and about to be transferred to Philadelphia, Smythe spoke to the civic pride of local investors and persuaded the team's owners to sell to a group he headed. Smythe soon changed the name of the team to the Maple Leafs to reflect his fierce patriotism and outfitted the team in his old University of Toronto colours: blue and white.

Smythe pioneered the idea of charting ice time, the plus-minus statistic, and filming games for review. If he was penurious with player salaries, he was absolutely of the time and many players found amenable summer work at his quarry. He was also a keen judge of ability. "If the Lord gave me any talents, it's the ability to smell a thoroughbred – either a human or a racehorse," he once said.

He was fiercely loyal to his Maple Leafs players. In 1933, as right winger Ace Bailey clung to life in a Boston hospital after a savage attack from Eddie Shore, Smythe held vigil outside the door of his room.

"He would find a way to help you out," said defenceman Bob Baun. "It was no different than when I started a big donnybrook with Chicago and I was fined $2,800. Conn sent my wife, Sally, a cheque for $2,800."

Smythe once said, "If I've done anything, I'd like to think I brought a little class to the game. It used to be that if you wanted to find a hockey player you had to go to a tavern or a beer hall. It's not like that today."

HARVEY "BUSHER" JACKSON

LEFT WING • 1929–30 TO 1938–39

Born: **January 19, 1911, Toronto, Ontario** Died: **June 25, 1966 (55), Toronto, Ontario**
Games: **432** Goals: **186** Assists: **165** Points: **351** PIMs: **342**
Stanley Cup: **1932**
Inducted into Hockey Hall of Fame: **1971**

Harvey "Busher" Jackson was an irresistible figure, the finesse on the legendary Kid Line, and a player whose skills were so arresting journalists tripped over themselves for superlatives. "He had everything," one reporter wrote. "Appearance, stature, speed, stickhandling ability, more shifts than a racing car and a blazing backhand shot." On the surface, it did seem like he had it all; but there was a shadow that followed him throughout his life.

Jackson got his nickname when he refused to help Leafs trainer Tim Daly cart some equipment bags. "You're nothing but a bush-leaguer [a minor leaguer], Jackson," came the friendly insult, and he was Busher forever after. In reality, he was anything but. Jackson was a four-time all-star, who at 21 was the youngest-ever player to lead the league in scoring. He once scored four goals in the third period of a game.

Jackson grew up playing on a frozen stretch in Toronto nicknamed Poverty Pond. When he made the NHL, he liked to flash his newfound prosperity and would keep a roll of money in his pocket for show. But success was fleeting and Conn Smythe traded him to the New York Rangers when Jackson was just 29. The former all-star was done by the age of 33.

There are differing views on Smythe's attitude toward Jackson. It is true that the Leafs owner paid some of Jackson's debts and found him

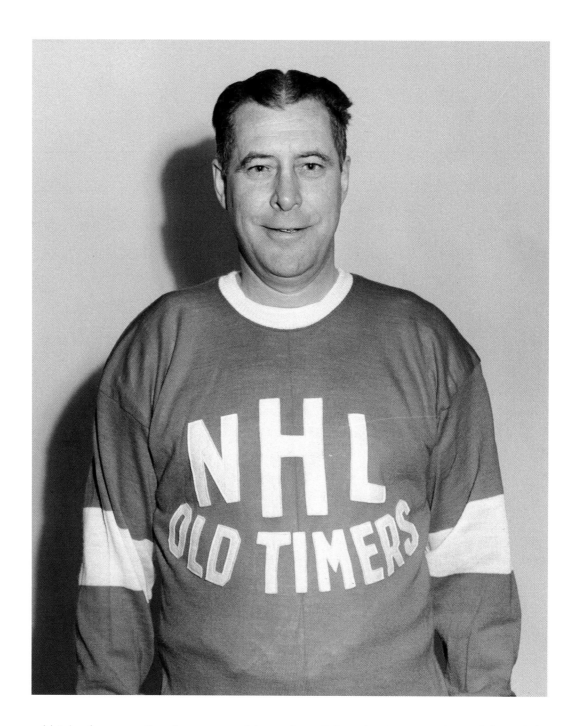

odd jobs; however, Smythe, a powerful member of the selection committee, did not help him attain the Hockey Hall of Fame.

Busher Jackson died at the age of 55 due to liver disease and the complications of a fall. In 1971, five years after his death, the Hall of Fame finally opened for Busher and he took his rightful place among his fellow hockey greats.

REGINALD "RED"
HORNER

DEFENCE • 1928–29 TO 1939–40

Born: **May 28, 1909, Lynden, Ontario** Died: **April 27, 2005 (95), Toronto, Ontario**
Games: **490** Goals: **42** Assists: **110** Points: **152** PIMs: **1,264**
Stanley Cup: **1932**

eginald "Red" Horner, the baddest of the Toronto Maple Leafs bad men, used to have an ominous slogan: "Do unto others before they do unto you."

When Conn Smythe took over the Maple Leafs, he could see his team was being easily bullied. He looked for a solution and found one right under his nose. Horner was familiar to Smythe's assistant general manager, Frank Selke, because the young man sometimes took an extra job as a delivery boy and had brought groceries to Selke's home. Smythe scouted a junior hockey game to see the 19-year-old prospect for himself.

"Mr. Smythe said, 'I'll tell you what I'm going to do,'" Horner recalled years later. "He said, 'I'll pay you $2,500 for the balance of the season.' I thought about it and it sounded pretty good because I was making $25 a week as a clerk at the Stock Exchange. We shook hands on the deal right there. No signing or anything, just a handshake."

Red Horner would go on to lead the league in penalty minutes for eight straight years. At six feet tall and 190 pounds, Horner was a big man for his time.

Hap Day (left) shaking hands with Red Horner in the Leafs dressing room

His courage on the ice led him to captain the Leafs for two years despite the presence of much more gifted players on the roster. A poor skater, Red Horner was a player the Major could admire, a relentless worker who protected his teammates like a mother hen. A very angry mother hen. When Eddie Shore ended Ace Bailey's career with a vicious hit from behind in 1933, it was Horner who responded by knocking Shore unconscious with a punch to the head.

Red Horner took the first shift seen at Maple Leaf Gardens when it opened in 1931. He was part of the closing ceremonies and on the ice when the Gardens closed in 1999.

HAROLD "BALDY"
COTTON

14

LEFT WING • 1928–29 TO 1934–35

Born: **November 5, 1902, Nanticoke, Ontario** Died: **September 9, 1984 (81), Toronto, Ontario**
Games: **285** Goals: **68** Assists: **88** Points: **156** PIMs: **252**
Stanley Cup: **1932**

E arly hair loss may have earned Harold Cotton his nickname, but it didn't stop him from being a television star.

Baldy Cotton spent seven years as a dependable left winger for the Leafs and another dozen seasons playing for the New York Americans. He was particularly prized as a penalty killer. "When you had [rambunctious defenceman] Red Horner on your team," Cotton once said, "you needed penalty killers." His off-ice career was twofold: he spent 25 years as a scout for the Boston Bruins, and during that time he was also a host on *Hockey Night in Canada*. The segment was called the "Hot Stove League," and it was his passport into the homes of countless scouting prospects.

"It was impossible to compete against the wealthy teams like Toronto and Montreal in those days, but one edge I had as a scout was my connection with the the "Hot Stove League," Cotton would later reminisce. "Any home I went into, even right to Vancouver, I was greeted by the parents like they had known me all their life."

Harold Cotton (right) and Hap Day (centre) at a Marlie Alumni game

Hockey teams are held together by camaraderie, mutual respect, and support – and a healthy dose of humour. This comes out in their nicknames, the dressing-room digs, and the pranks they play on each other. Baldy Cotton was notoriously afraid of heights and was the subject of one of the Leafs' more hair-raising pranks when Charlie Conacher held him by his ankles out the 20th floor window of a Manhattan hotel.

Cotton spied a 14-year-old defenceman from Parry Sound in a minor hockey game played in Unionville, a suburb of Toronto. The next week, every member of the Boston organization, at Cotton's insistence, watched his next game. The Bruins launched a sustained and eventually successful wooing of the prospect, a young kid with a brush-cut named Bobby Orr.

IRVINE "ACE"
BAILEY

RIGHT WING • 1926–27 TO 1933–34

Born: **July 3, 1903, Bracebridge, Ontario** Died: **April 7, 1992 (88), Toronto, Ontario**
Games: **313** Goals: **111** Assists: **82** Points: **193** PIMs: **472**
Stanley Cup: **1932**
Inducted into Hockey Hall of Fame: **1975**

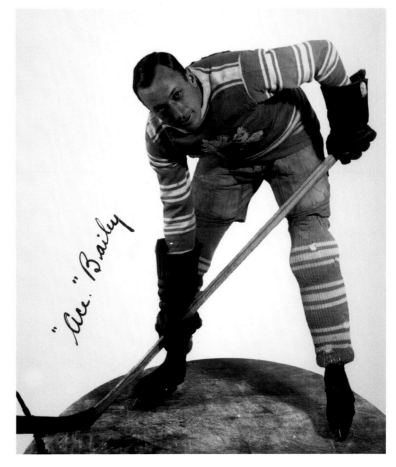

A ce Bailey was an excellent all-around player and penalty killer and led the league in scoring in the 1928–29 season. After only four seasons, his career would come to an end in one of hockey's most famous fights.

It was during a December 1933 game against the hometown Bruins when King Clancy, the Leafs' bantamweight defenceman, tripped the Bruins' legendary bad man Eddie Shore. Shore was in a foul mood. The Leafs were a far superior team and seemed to be toying with the Bruins. Shore had just rejoined the team after an acrimonious contract dispute.

Clancy loved to rush the puck, so as Shore gathered himself up, Bailey dropped back into Clancy's position. Looking up, Shore only saw Bailey's back and, thinking it was Bailey who brought him down, hurled himself into the back of the defenceless Leafs winger. Bailey's head hit the ice, fracturing his skull. In the ensuing melée, Leafs defenceman Red Horner returned the favour and knocked Shore momentarily unconscious. Bailey would regain consciousness in the

Ace Bailey and Boston's Eddie Shore shake hands on March 6, 1934

dressing room, ask to go back in, and then collapse again.

He was in a coma for 15 days. Newspapers prepared obituaries, and Conn Smythe convened a vigil outside his hospital room, ordering his assistant general manager, Frank Selke, to prepare to return the body to Toronto.

Bailey's father vowed to kill the man who had injured his son and took a train to Boston armed with a handgun. He stopped in a bar to gather his courage, and a local policeman, tipped to the father's presence by Leafs officials, disarmed the man and sent him home.

While in a coma, Bailey was operated on twice and finally recovered enough to be released from hospital. But Ace Bailey would never play again. It was a tragedy felt throughout the sport. In recognition of this loss, an all-star benefit game at the Gardens, the first of its kind, was organized later that year in his honour. Before the game's greatest stars were introduced, Bailey and Shore shook hands. Leafs owner Conn Smythe announced to the crowd that no other Leaf would wear Bailey's number 6. This was the first time in professional sports that a number was retired in recognition of an athlete's contribution to his game.

Smythe found work for Bailey as a timekeeper at the Gardens, and there he stayed for 47 years. Bailey loved the work ethic displayed by Leafs winger Ron Ellis and requested the number be reinstated for Ellis's use.

"I held no grudge," Bailey said later. "It was something that can happen in the heat of the battle. It's like anything else. Sometimes you say something in anger and regret it." Even though Ace Bailey only stood a reedy five foot ten, he was a big, big man. He was a giant among the Leafs because of one simple gesture: he shook the hand of the man who had ended his NHL career.

When he died at 88 in 1992, Bailey was the oldest surviving Leaf. "This was not," the *Toronto Star* dryly noted, "the first obituary written about Ace Bailey."

FOSTER HEWITT

Born: **November 21, 1902, Toronto, Ontario** Died: **April 21, 1985 (82), Toronto, Ontario**
Inducted into Hockey Hall of Fame: **1965 (Builder)**

There was no question; it was going to be a terribly long day for the young *Toronto Star* reporter. Foster Hewitt had been asked to cover a prominent junior hockey playoff game between Toronto Parkdale and Kitchener after a full day working on other sports stories. Bill Hewitt, the *Star*'s sports editor (and Foster's father), had no interest in the new technology with which the newspaper was experimenting. For the committed newspaperman, the concept of radio seemed out of this world. But his son had no hesitation.

March 22, 1923, went down in history as Foster Hewitt's first hockey broadcast. A telephone was rigged up to a rail seat near the penalty box of the old Mutual Street Arena. It was where he was sitting when one of the teams scored. The young reporter intoned, "He shoots. He scores." The definitive phrase of the hockey lexicon had been ushered into the world. "It just seemed the thing to say," Hewitt would later remember. "I didn't have time to think how I was going to say things and just described what I was seeing on the ice. I didn't make any changes in that approach over the next fifty or so years."

When Conn Smythe landed control of the Leafs in 1927, he installed a box high up in the Mutual Street rafters from which Hewitt could work. Later, when he built Maple Leaf Gardens, a grateful Smythe, who used Hewitt's new medium to round up financiers, instructed Hewitt to design his own perch. Hewitt spent three hours one day walking up and down the stairs of a building, looking out various windows to decide what level offered the best view. He decided on the fifth floor. Smythe dutifully installed the rafters of the arena five floors (17 metres/56 feet) from the ice.

Securing a radio booth that high up meant the only way to reach it would be by catwalk. The trip to the "gondola," named by a radio engineer who thought the tiny booth reminiscent of the passenger compartments in Zeppelins, demanded a spartan fearlessness. Hewitt himself was too frightened to ever look down while crossing the catwalk.

Foster Hewitt was the voice of the Maple Leafs from coast to coast

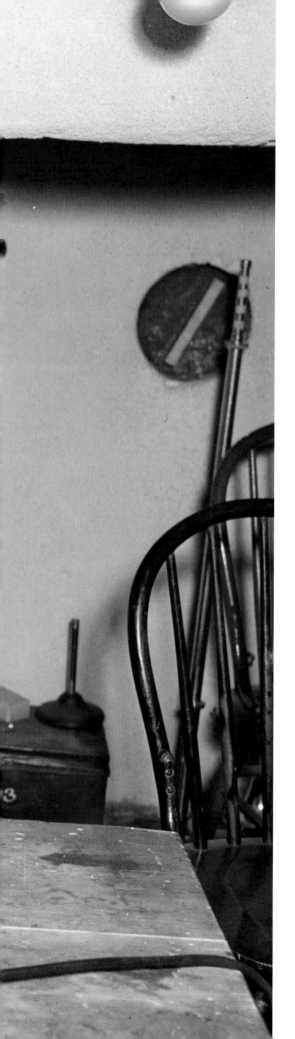

Radio made Foster Hewitt a wealthy man and the most famous Maple Leaf to work without skates. *Hockey Night in Canada*, which existed solely as a radio product for 21 years, made the Leafs a household name and a welcome guest in residences across the country.

On a barnstorming tour of western Canada, star winger Charlie Conacher was struck by the crowds of well-wishers who wanted to see Foster Hewitt in the flesh. Introduced along with the players, Hewitt was always recorded a thunderous hand.

"The biggest ovation and most attention did not go to a big, burly hockey player," Conacher said. "It went to a little guy who never scored a goal ... Foster Hewitt."

The technological advantage of radio echoes to this day. Cheering for the Leafs became a family tradition, and today the team has fifth-generation fans scattered all over Canada.

"Foster Hewitt," said Smythe, "made every Canadian boy want to be a Maple Leaf."

Left to right: Charlie Conacher, Joe Primeau, and Busher Jackson – the Kid Line

THE 1930s

JAMES DICKINSON "DICK" IRVIN

FRANCIS MICHAEL "KING" CLANCY

JOE PRIMEAU

CHARLIE CONACHER

RUDOLPH "BINGO" KAMPMAN

TEAM OF THE DECADE
1931–32 TORONTO MAPLE LEAFS, STANLEY CUP CHAMPIONS

REGULAR SEASON RECORD: 23-18-7
PLAYOFF RECORD: 5-1-1

The Leafs' 1932 three-game sweep of the New York Rangers in the Stanley Cup final was notable for three elements: First, the Leafs clinched the Cup in the newly christened Maple Leaf Gardens. Second, the Leafs claimed the title despite making a coaching change in the early going with Art Duncan sacked in favour of Dick Irvin, who would win his only Cup as a Leafs coach. Third, because the circus was booked in Madison Square Garden, the Rangers surrendered their home-ice advantage and instead played Game 3 at Boston Garden, where the Leafs triumphed easily by a score of 4–2.

These were the glory days for the famed Kid Line of Charlie Conacher, Joe Primeau, and Harvey "Busher" Jackson. Jackson led the NHL with 53 points in 48 games. The elegant Primeau likewise led the league with 37 assists. Charlie Conacher led the league in goals with 34. It would mark the only time in the team's history that a different Leaf led the league in goals, assists, and points. The defence was anchored by King Clancy, who enjoyed a 10-goal season, and Red Horner, who, as was his habit, led the league in penalty minutes.

The Leafs blasted the Chicago Black Hawks by an aggregate of 6–2 in total goals for the series and narrowly beat the Montreal Maroons 4–3 in another total-goals final to set up the sweep of the Rangers. The Kid Line produced eight of the Leafs' 18 goals in the final. Toronto boasted seven eventual Hall of Famers in Jackson, Primeau, Conacher, Horner, Hap Day, Ace Bailey, and King Clancy.

Dick Irvin as the first captain for the Chicago Black Hawks in their inaugural NHL season in 1926–27

JAMES DICKINSON "DICK"
IRVIN

COACH • 1931–40

Born: **January 19, 1892, Hamilton, Ontario** Died: **May 15, 1957 (64), Montreal, Quebec**
Games: **426** Record: **215 W, 152 L, 59 T** Pts. %: **.574**
Stanley Cup: **1932**
Inducted into Hockey Hall of Fame: **1958 (Builder)**

Dick Irvin was serious and sombre, the perfect counterpoint to Conn Smythe, his mentor, rival, and antagonist. Irvin spent 50 years in hockey, and he got his start with Smythe. That partnership, with Smythe as the iron-willed overseer and manager and Irvin as the occasionally rebellious but equally doctrinaire coach, would produce a Stanley Cup for the Leafs in 1932.

Irvin made the league as a 34-year-old rookie and toiled for three seasons in the NHL before a skull fracture ended his playing career. Smythe, convinced that coach Art Duncan didn't rule with the necessary authority, tapped Irvin, and what would become an eight-year odyssey with the Leafs took flight.

Many of the players didn't know who Irvin was, but it was clear he had an immediate impact when the Leafs took part in a bench-clearing brawl in his first game. From that day forward, Smythe would never doubt Irvin's ability to motivate players.

They made the oddest of couples. Smythe was the "Major." He barked orders, chewed out subordinates, and issued proclamations. Irvin was an innovator but colourless. Newspapers would come to call him the "Gloomy Dean" of NHL coaches.

But it was Dick Irvin who popularized the three-line format, and the wave of fresh attackers the Leafs regularly unfurled stymied opponents.

Conn Smythe (right) and now-rival Montreal coach Dick Irvin Sr., November 13, 1945, at Maple Leaf Gardens

Many teams couldn't afford the talent to stock three separate units, and the Leafs profited through Smythe's largesse and Irvin's inventiveness. In one playoff series, Irvin rotated goalies to keep his team sharp and his opponents confused. Critics said it worked the other way around. Irvin began a practice of grading each player's performance after every game. Temperate but decisive, Irvin once said, "I have long been disposed to judge men by their average. If it is reasonably high, I am charitable with faults that look black."

Irvin's coaching style and strategies live on: they have become standard among modern-day coaches.

FRANCIS MICHAEL "KING"
CLANCY

DEFENCE • 1930–31 TO 1936–37
COACH • 1953–56, 1966–67, 1971–72

Born: **February 25, 1903, Ottawa, Ontario** Died: **November 10, 1986 (83), Toronto, Ontario**
Games (player): **286** Goals: **52** Assists: **78** Points: **130** PIMs: **383**
Games (coach): **206** Record: **80 W, 81 L, 49 T** Pts. %: **.498**
Stanley Cup: **1932 (player)**
Inducted into Hockey Hall of Fame: **1958**

K ing Clancy was the Maple Leafs' first great star, the player who set the bar for all those to come. He was also an impossible act to follow. Clancy led the Leafs to their 1931–32 Cup. He would twice be named a first all-star, and he captured second all-star status twice as well.

In 1930, Conn Smythe paid the unheard of sum of $35,000 and two players to land a five-foot-seven, 140-pound defenceman who never won a fight. "Couldn't fight a lick," Smythe once said, "but he never backed up."

The story of how Smythe came to land Clancy is a part of Leafs lore. Looking for a marquee talent for his newly acquired team, Smythe bet the little cash he had on a horse called Rare Jewel, a mare that would post its only career win on the day of Smythe's bet. Smythe took his winnings, borrowed another $20,000, and landed Clancy.

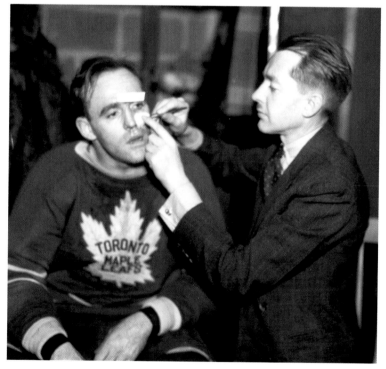

King Clancy getting patched up

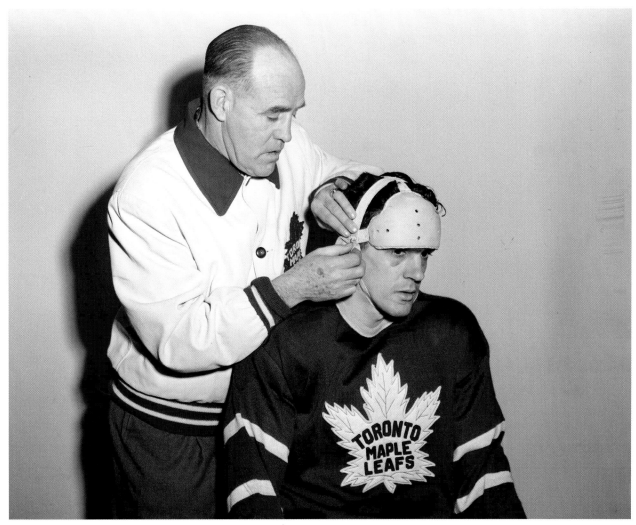

Coach King Clancy adjusts headgear – but not a complete helmet – for Hugh Bolton

Clancy would coach the Leafs three times, spend 11 years as the league's most colourful referee, and then settle in to a long stint as the team's kindly good luck charm. In all, he worked for the Leafs for 56 years. "What is it you do here?" Punch Imlach would puckishly ask Clancy, knowing full well that Clancy had no real job but immense standing as an unofficial ambassador, a foil for the bombastic Harold Ballad, and a link to the first days of the franchise.

King Clancy died in November 1986 at the age of 83, and his funeral procession included a slow pass in front of Maple Leaf Gardens, where staff lined the sidewalk for one final moment with the King.

"What a man," said his longtime teammate Baldy Cotton. "The life of every party and a player who was so good he seemed to be able to score whenever he wanted to."

7 JOE PRIMEAU

  CENTRE • 1927–28 TO 1935–36
COACH • 1950–53

Born: **January 29, 1906, Lindsay, Ontario** Died: **May 14, 1989 (83), Toronto, Ontario**
Games (player): **310** Goals: **66** Assists: **177** Points: **243** PIMs: **105**
Games (coach): **210** Record: **97 W, 71 L, 42 T** Pts. %: **.562**
Stanley Cup: **1932 (player), 1951 (coach)**
Awards: **Lady Byng Trophy, 1932**
Inducted into Hockey Hall of Fame: **1963**

They called him "Gentleman Joe," a top centreman who averaged just half-a-dozen minor penalties in his eight full seasons with the club. Primeau was the hub of the Kid Line, a Leafs unit that roared through the Dirty Thirties and, through the magic of Foster Hewitt's radio broadcasts, entranced a nation of fans, most of whom had never seen the Leafs in person.

After being fired by the New York Rangers, Conn Smythe made Joe Primeau the first player he brought to Toronto. Primeau's genial nature hid a fiery competitiveness. One New Year's Eve in New York, Primeau was highsticked late in the game and lost a whole row of teeth. He personally scoured the city looking for help until he ran into a drunken dentist who patched him up.

Primeau later coached the Leafs for three years and won a Cup before retiring to the business world, where he ran a successful company that manufactured

Joe Primeau giving pointers

bricks for builders. He never lost his love for the game, and even decades after his retirement as a player, Primeau would be asked into the Leafs dressing room to meet a new generation of players.

A wise and wry man, Primeau appreciated the attention but understood the nature of hockey players.

"If I went into the Leafs dressing room today, they'd look at me and say, 'Ahh, who does that old guy think he is, talking about how great the oldtimers played.' They think the game started when they came along."

"It's funny," said the great Joe Primeau. "So did we."

CHARLIE CONACHER

RIGHT WING • 1929–30 TO 1937–38

Born: **December 20, 1909, Toronto, Ontario** Died: **December 30, 1967 (58), Toronto, Ontario**
Games: **326** Goals: **200** Assists: **124** Points: **324** PIMs: **411**
Stanley Cup: **1932**
Inducted into Hockey Hall of Fame: **1961**

Chas. W. Conacher

One day, while a junior Elmwood Millionaires goalie named Lyall Holmes was preparing for a game against the Toronto Marlboros, a teammate warned him about a hard-shooting winger named Charlie Conacher.

Holmes was a confident, experienced goalie, but no amount of preparation could prepare him for what was to come.

"Conacher almost killed me with his first shot," Holmes would say later. "I saw this big kid crossing our blueline and without any warning he dipped his wrists. I didn't even see the shot, just a blur out of the corner of my left eye, and I ducked my head instinctively. The puck hit me on the back of the head. I woke up, feeling my face, lying on the ice. If that puck would have hit me on the temple, it would have killed me."

Such was the power of the man they would come to call the "Big Blue Bomber." Holmes was sounding a warning for all the goalies to come.

Charlie Conacher was the most arresting figure on the dominant line of his era, the Kid Line. Radio announcer Foster Hewitt brought the Kid Line into living rooms all across Canada and, in doing so, made Charlie Conacher an almost mythical figure.

If Joe Primeau was the elegant architect and Busher Jackson the talented whiz kid, Conacher was the driving force, a player so charismatic you can sustain a good argument that he was the Leafs' best-ever right winger.

From left: Charlie Conacher, Joe Primeau, and Ace Bailey on November 11, 1953

Conacher played nine seasons with the Leafs before the injuries that came with his courageous play finally grounded him. He broke 30 goals four times and won the league's scoring title in 1933–34 and 1935–36. He led the league or tied for the league lead in goals six times and was a three-time first all-star.

Perhaps this ending wasn't so surprising given that Conacher came from one of Canada's most distinguished, though poor, athletic families. He shares Hockey Hall of Fame honours with his older brother Lionel and younger brother Roy.

"We didn't have a pretzel. We didn't have enough money to buy toothpaste," he once said.

He sharpened his games practising endlessly on a neighbourhood outdoor rink.

"I just about lived on that rink," Conacher said. "I practised shooting the puck against the boards for hours, and I mean for hours. I skated until I thought my legs would drop off. Even when I made the Leafs, I kept at it."

"The Kid Line offered relief from the sorrow and desperation a worldwide depression had created," wrote *Toronto Star* columnist Milt Dunnell. "If three young men could come of the ponds, the open air rinks and the frozen creeks to command international attention, there was hope for the man whose modest ambition was to find a job."

Conacher would become wildly successful in the hotel and oil businesses, but throat cancer would still the Big Blue Bomber at 58.

"The fondest memories I have of Charlie were the ones that found us scrounging apples off other people's trees or getting a freshly-baked loaf of bread from Canada Bread," wrote longtime friend Red Burnett of the *Star*. "We'd dig out the doughy centre, pack the cavity with butter and what a treat. That was my Conacher, leader and champion of the poor sweats who knew what it was to be hungry and without a dime."

Bingo Kampman (left) and Bucko McDonald, January 6, 1942

RULDOPH "BINGO" KAMPMAN

DEFENCE • 1937–38 TO 1941–42

Born: **March 12, 1914, Berlin, Ontario** Died: **December 22, 1987 (73), St. Mary's, Ontario**
Games: **189** Goals: **14** Assists: **30** Points: **44** PIMs: **287**
Stanley Cup: **1942**

Bingo Kampman was so strong he won pocket money by betting he could lift up the ends of tables … with his teeth. A rugged bodychecker, his nickname was said to have come from the cries of spectators when Kampman lowered his shoulder and drove an opposing player into the boards. His power was packed into just five feet nine inches and 180 pounds.

Kampman, a defensive specialist, was often paired with hard-rock rearguard Red Horner. Kampman spent his entire career, 189 regular season games and 43 more in the playoffs, with the Maple Leafs and like many sacrificed his career to the Second World War. Kampman played in Game 7 of the 1942 Stanley Cup final, a playoff made famous by a furious Leafs comeback that saw them win four straight games after dropping the first three to the Detroit Red Wings.

Kampman enlisted a few days after the Cup win. He was part of a flotilla of Leafs that included the Metz brothers, Don and Nick; Johnny McCreedy; Wally Stanowski; Ernie Dickens; and Bob Goldham. Thankfully, all returned alive. By the time the war ended, Bingo Kampman was 31, and while he would play in the American League and in senior leagues, his NHL career would endure as an example of a Leaf who sacrificed his own prospects for an infinitely greater cause.

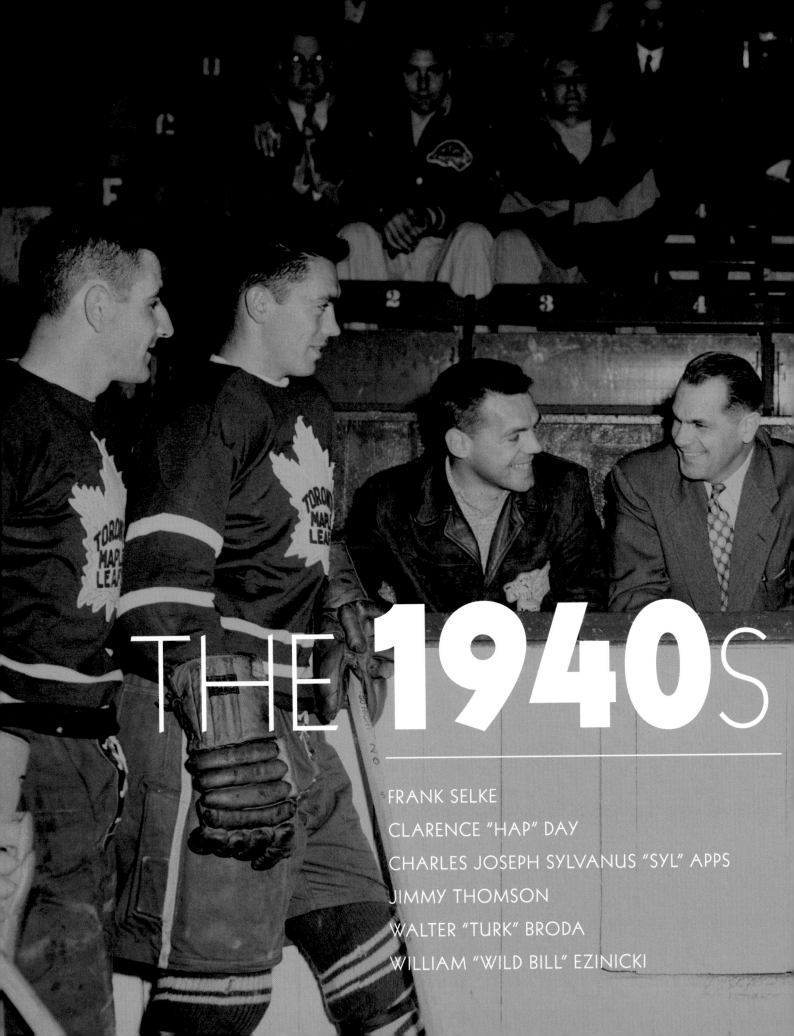

THE 1940s

FRANK SELKE

CLARENCE "HAP" DAY

CHARLES JOSEPH SYLVANUS "SYL" APPS

JIMMY THOMSON

WALTER "TURK" BRODA

WILLIAM "WILD BILL" EZINICKI

From left: George Armstrong, Howie Meeker, Syl Apps, Hap Day, Harry Watson, Ted Kennedy, and Jimmy Thomson

TEAM OF THE DECADE
1947–48 TORONTO MAPLE LEAFS, STANLEY CUP CHAMPIONS

REGULAR SEASON RECORD: 32-15-13

PLAYOFF RECORD: 8-1

The 1940s brought five Stanley Cups to Toronto, but the 1948 Cup champs might have been the best in the club's history. The Leafs finished first in the NHL with a 32-15-13 record and then raced through the Stanley Cup final, beating Boston 4–1 and then sweeping Detroit, including a 7–2 Cup-clinching victory in Motown. In one of his most brilliant moves, Conn Smythe traded five players to Chicago to land 27-year-old centreman Max Bentley in November 1947.

"I learned how to win in Toronto," Bentley would later say, and he dazzled in the playoffs, finishing first in assists with 11 and second in points behind Ted Kennedy.

The Leafs boasted a trio of Hall of Fame centremen in Syl Apps, Kennedy, and Bentley, and Smythe pegged the 1948 club as the strongest-ever Leafs team because of the club's devastating talent at centre. Hall of Fame left winger Harry Watson won the second of four Stanley Cups with the Leafs and scored 26 goals in the regular season and four more in the nine playoff games.

Goalie Turk Broda, another eventual Hall of Famer, surrendered a scant 2.15 goals a game. The defence was anchored by elegant Jimmy Thomson, and the team's feared tough guy, Wild Bill Ezinicki, chipped in with three post-season goals. The 1948 final represented the third and final Stanley Cup for the great Apps, who retired at 33.

FRANK SELKE

  ASSISTANT GENERAL MANAGER • 1929–46

Born: **May 7, 1893, Berlin, Ontario** Died: **July 3, 1985 (92), Rigaud, Quebec**

Stanley Cups: **1932, 1942, 1945**

Inducted into Hockey Hall of Fame: **1960 (Builder)**

Frank Selke (left) and King Clancy

As a young man in Berlin, Ontario, Frank Selke organized amateur hockey teams while he worked as a tradesman.

Conn Smythe, whose eye for management talent rivalled his ability to recognize able hockey players, ran into Selke when they were both operating amateur hockey teams and tapped him to help him run the Maple Leafs. He called Selke "The Little Electrician."

The fiery Smythe and the taciturn Selke were an often fractious pairing, but they were perfectly cast. Selke was level-headed enough to endure Smythe's sometimes outlandish demands, and Smythe shrewdly recognized Selke's enormous organizational talents. While Selke was never credited with the role of general manager, he and Smythe operated in concert from 1929–46, a span that saw the Leafs win three Stanley Cups.

Selke is the father of hockey's farm system, which tied up vast numbers of talented players fighting their way up the ranks. At one point in his career, six of his teams were simultaneously contending for the Memorial Cup. He was so shrewd that while operating the Montreal

Frank Selke (left) and Rocket Richard

Canadiens he bought an entire league, the Quebec Senior Hockey League, to acquire one player: a star with the Quebec Aces named Jean Beliveau. The Little Electrician operated with an engineer's clear vision. "If you improve management in every rink," he once said, "you improve hockey in every rink."

Selke's relationship with Smythe soured when, with Smythe fighting overseas in the Second World War, Selke acquired a prospect named Ted Kennedy for a veteran of some ability named Frankie Eddolls. While Smythe would revere Kennedy, he began to suspect Selke of an unforgiveable offence … a lack of loyalty. Whispers began to reach him about Selke's widening circle of influence, and there were rumours that team directors would favour installing Selke over Smythe.

Selke was an invaluable employee, living up to his letterhead, which read, "There is no substitute for quality." His union connections proved essential in convincing tradespeople to work for lower wages for a share of Gardens stock. But there would be no reconciling the two men, and Selke resigned, ending a 17-year partnership that helped establish and define the organization.

Near the end of Selke's life, a newspaperman asked Selke what he would tell the modern-day player. "You can't tell them anything," said The Little Electrician. "The good ones don't have to be told and the bad ones don't want to be told."

Toronto Coach Hap Day behind the bench, November 2, 1946,
Maple Leaf Gardens

CLARENCE "HAP" DAY

DEFENCE • 1924–25 TO 1936–37 **C** 🏒 🏆
COACH • 1940–50

Born: **June 14, 1901, Owen Sound, Ontario** Died: **February 17, 1990 (88), St. Thomas, Ontario**
Games (player): **538** Goals: **86** Assists: **113** Points: **199** PIMs: **587**
Games (coach): **210** Record: **259 W, 206 L, 81 T** Pts. %: **.549**
Stanley Cups: **1932 (player), 1942, 1945, 1947, 1948, 1949 (coach)**
Inducted into Hockey Hall of Fame: **1961**

Nicknamed "Happy" as a child for his bright, cheerful countenance, Hap Day pioneered the black art of the clutch and grab as a longtime Leafs defenceman. It was Day who first conceived the idea of hollowing out his gloves to make it easier to grab the jersey of an opposing forward. He brought a brilliant overall game. While defencemen of his era rarely wandered over the opposing blueline, Day was a daring rusher who managed 62 goals and 161 points in 11 Leafs seasons.

An original Maple Leaf, Day captained the first Stanley Cup–winning team in 1932. His 10-year term as team captain trailed only that of George Armstrong and Mats Sundin. But it was as a coach that Hap Day truly shone. When Day took over for Dick Irvin as coach of the Leafs, he had no NHL coaching experience, but he was the architect of the franchise's defence-first philosophy.

Hap Day celebrating after Game 4 of the Stanley Cup final, April 16, 1949, Maple Leaf Gardens

The Maple Leafs' D: Bingo Kampman, Bucko McDonald, Ernie Dickens, Wally Stanowski (kneeling), Bob Goldham, and coach Hap Day, March 20, 1942

Day's knowledge of the rule book was so encyclopedic that he frequently sent one as a gift to King Clancy, once his defence partner but later the NHL's most flamboyant official. Day's instructions to Clancy were succinct: "Read It."

His teams were always superbly prepared. A master of the faceoff, Day drilled the importance of the draw into his team. Day's Leafs teams, four of which were captained by the inspirational Ted Kennedy, won championships in 1942, 1945, 1947, 1948, and 1949. Only Scotty Bowman (nine Cups) and Toe Blake (eight) won more Stanley Cups than Hap Day.

SYLVANUS "SYL" APPS

CENTRE • 1936–37 TO 1942–43/1945–46 TO 1947–48

Born: **January 18, 1915, Paris, Ontario** Died: **December 24, 1998 (83), Kingston, Ontario**
Games: **423** Goals: **201** Assists: **231** Points: **432** PIMs: **56**
Stanley Cups: **1942, 1947, 1948**
Awards: **Calder Trophy, 1937; Lady Byng Trophy, 1942**
Inducted into Hockey Hall of Fame: **1961**

Syl Apps was famous for his skating, even if most of the people who recognized him as one of the fastest, most elegant players in the NHL never saw him take a stride. Apps, who played for the Maple Leafs from 1936 to 1948, starred in the era of radio. He was a word-of-mouth superstar. Journalists who did see him struggled to find adequate superlatives. *Sport Magazine* called him Rembrandt on ice and rhapsodized, "He plays with such grace and precision you get the impression that every move is the execution of a mental image conveyed long before he went through the actions."

Apps grew up in Paris, Ontario, two hours from Toronto, the son of a prosperous druggist who flooded a low spot of the family property every winter to create a skating rink for his kids. Apps quickly perfected his stride through long days and nights on the rink. His skating was so powerful that at 14 he played in junior hockey against players as old as 20. He graduated from Paris High School as valedictorian at 16 and starred as a pole vaulter who would compete in 1934 for Canada at the Olympics in Berlin.

Conn Smythe first spied Apps on the football field and reasoned that anyone that athletic on the gridiron would be a natural on the ice. While he relished hard-hitting hockey, Smythe also valued an upscale clientele. Apps was a gentlemanly player who once went a season without a penalty. He also had the fire to win that Smythe demanded.

From left: Syl Apps scores the overtime winning goal during Game 1 of the Stanley Cup quarterfinal, March 19, 1940, Maple Leaf Gardens. Toronto defeated Chicago 3–2

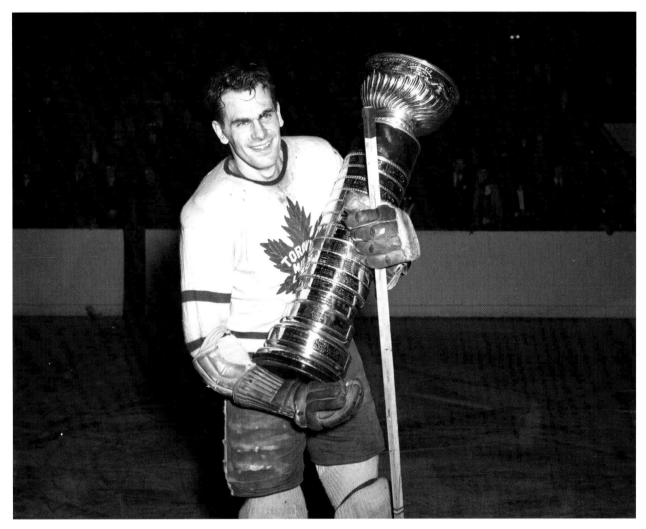
Syl Apps after Game 7 of the Stanley Cup final series, April 18, 1942. Toronto beat Detroit 3–1

"He never would go out to hurt anybody, but he played to win every night," said longtime linemate Bob Davidson.

Toward the end of his playing career, Apps felt he had given hockey everything he could. He told Smythe he wanted to retire at the end of the 1947–48 season, but Smythe convinced him to stick around to score his 200th career goal. On the last night of the season, Apps notched a hat trick in Detroit to finish with 201. He retired at 33, even though his 26 goals and 53 points were career highs. Syl Apps, the only Maple Leafs centre ever chosen as a first-team all-star, won three Stanley Cups in the six years he captained the team.

Apps would go on to enjoy a long term in politics and was revered by those who knew him, just as he had been, thanks to the power of radio, by those who had only heard of him.

"He was as fine a man as ever lived," said teammate and protege Ted "Teeder" Kennedy. "Besides being a great player, he was as good a man as there was off the ice. He set the standard other players would do well to follow."

From left: captain Ted Kennedy, Turk Broda, Max Bentley, and Jimmy Thomson (with a black eye)

JIMMY THOMSON

DEFENCE • 1945–46 TO 1956–57 🏆

Born: **February 23, 1927, Winnipeg, Manitoba** Died: **May 18, 1991 (64), Toronto, Ontario**
Games: **717** Goals: **15** Assists: **208** Points: **223** PIMs: **845**
Stanley Cups: **1947, 1948, 1949, 1951**

One of the most underrated defensive rearguards in franchise history, Jimmy Thomson was the heart of the Leafs defensive corps in the mid-1940s and early 1950s and the defensive conscience of a team that won four Stanley Cups between 1947 and 1951.

The Leafs put the Winnipeg native on their blueline as a 19-year-old, and from the beginning, Thomson showed little interest in scoring. He had six seasons in the NHL without a goal, but with Thomson backing him up, flashy, mustachioed Gus Mortson was free to roam. Newspaper people called the pair the Gold Dust Twins. Thomson was the embodiment of the clutch-and-grab, slow-the-opposition style favoured by Leafs coach Hap Day. A second all-star in 1950–51, Thomson was accorded the captaincy in 1956–57 but returned the letter when Ted Kennedy came out of retirement.

Thomson would have retired as one of the Leafs' most dependable rearguards but for an off-ice incident that enraged Leafs founder Conn Smythe. A group of players, spearheaded by Detroit's Ted Lindsay and Montreal defenceman Doug Harvey, wanted information about how the players' pension money was being invested. Far from a union, the players called their new organization an association, but Smythe despised unions and the principals were quickly traded. Lindsay, like Thomson, soon found himself dealt to the Black Hawks. Thomson played one season in Chicago and then retired to a successful business career. A seven-time all-star and four-time Stanley Cup champ, Thomson remains one of the most unheralded but accomplished Leafs in franchise history.

Jimmy Thomson (right) and Gus Mortson, the sensational rookie rearguard duo, December 1946, Maple Leaf Gardens

Turk Broda eating pancakes in net for a promotional stunt

WALTER "TURK" BRODA

GOALTENDER • 1936–37 TO 1942–43/1945–46 TO 1951–52

Born: **May 15, 1914, Brandon, Manitoba** Died: **October 17, 1972 (58), Toronto, Ontario**
Games: **629** Wins: **302** Losses: **224** Ties: **101** Shutouts: **62** Goals against: **2.53**
Stanley Cups: **1942, 1947, 1948, 1949, 1951**
Awards: **Vezina Trophy, 1941, 1948**
Inducted into Hockey Hall of Fame: **1967**

When Turk Broda died, Toronto sportswriter Gary Lautens wrote of the Leafs goalie: "When the playoff bucks were on the line, the Turk could catch lint in a hurricane."

That was the legacy of the great Turk Broda, the Leafs' greatest clutch goalie. Broda won more regular season games (302) and recorded more shutouts (62) than any other Leafs goalie. He was even better in the playoffs, where he established unbreakable standards for post-season wins (with 60) and Stanley Cups by a goalie (with five). Broda had a lifetime regular season goals against average of 2.53, but in the playoffs he shrank his aggregate to a phenomenal 1.99.

Broda had a stock answer for his bloodless play in the post-season. "For one thing, I always needed the money," he said, "but it probably was a case of me being too dumb to realize how serious it was. I never let the pressure get to me."

He was as competitive as any goalie to prowl the Leafs crease and was especially locked in after games in which the Leafs had lost or he had played poorly.

Turk Broda holds the pig gifted to him by Conn Smythe as part of a Christmas party joke, December 23, 1951

Turk Broda with the 1941 Vezina Trophy

"Nobody had the flair that Turk had to come back after a bad game and play superlatively," said Conn Smythe.

His nickname came from his complexion. A childhood friend said Broda's freckled face was as spotted as a turkey egg and the world would forevermore know Walter as "Turk." Journalists later graced him with another nickname. In 1950, Broda's weight hit the headlines when Smythe pronounced him too fat to play. At five foot nine and 200 pounds, Broda was never really corpulent, but his weight was a staple of the sports pages — they called him the "Fabulous Fat Man." Fans mailed in hundreds of diets.

"It was great stuff, a million laughs," he said once. "Funny thing was, I never lost an ounce."

WILLIAM "WILD BILL" EZINICKI

RIGHT WING • 1944–45 TO 1949–50

Born: **March 11, 1924, Winnipeg, Manitoba** Died: **October 11, 2012 (88), Gloucester, Massachusetts**
Games: **271** Goals: **56** Assists: **79** Points: **135** PIMs: **525**
Stanley Cups: **1947, 1948, 1949**

B ill Ezinicki won three Stanley Cups and played seven seasons with the Leafs. At five foot ten and 170 pounds, Ezinicki was famous for his strength, which he cultivated as one of the few players of his era to lift weights.

He undertook 368 NHL games, but his best years were with the Leafs, for whom he played six seasons. His credo was simple enough: "If you're wearing the other guy's uniform," said Wild Bill Ezinicki, "then you're the enemy." Wild Bill was one of the toughest players of his era. Rumours circulated he had an insurance policy that paid him $5 a stitch, and he once scored a winning goal for the Leafs a few shifts after losing four teeth. So reviled was Wild Bill Ezinicki in the other five NHL cities that he was once stabbed in the rear by a woman brandishing a sharp pin used to secure her hat. His bodycheck of New York Ranger Edgar Laprade in 1947 was so devastating the Rangers sought to have Ezinicki barred for the safety of players throughout the league.

Despite the Rangers' protests, most agreed that Wild Bill lived on the right side of the line.

Leafs in off-ice training in the early 1950s. Bill Ezinicki is front, left

The Leafs and New York Rangers settling their differences. Bill Ezinicki is the Leaf holding the Ranger along the boards

"He's a tough little guy," appraised Montreal's Hall of Fame defenceman Ken Reardon. "He's definitely not dirty. He can check and pester and sometimes hurt you. He makes you mad, but he's not dirty."

Upon retirement, Wild Bill was just known as Bill, a tremendous golf pro who routinely played in the top open tournaments in the United States. But while he chose a gentler vocation, Bill Ezinicki never went soft even late in life. After a burglar, thinking the Ezinicki house was empty, came upon Wild Bill, police were called to collect the offender. There was one detour: the thief had to be taken to the hospital for stitches. Wild Bill Ezinicki had struck again.

From left: Coach Joe Primeau, Howie Meeker, Cal Gardner, Bill Barilko, Bill Juzda, Harry Watson, and Joe Klukay celebrating Barilko's Stanley Cup–winning overtime goal in Game 5, April 21, 1951

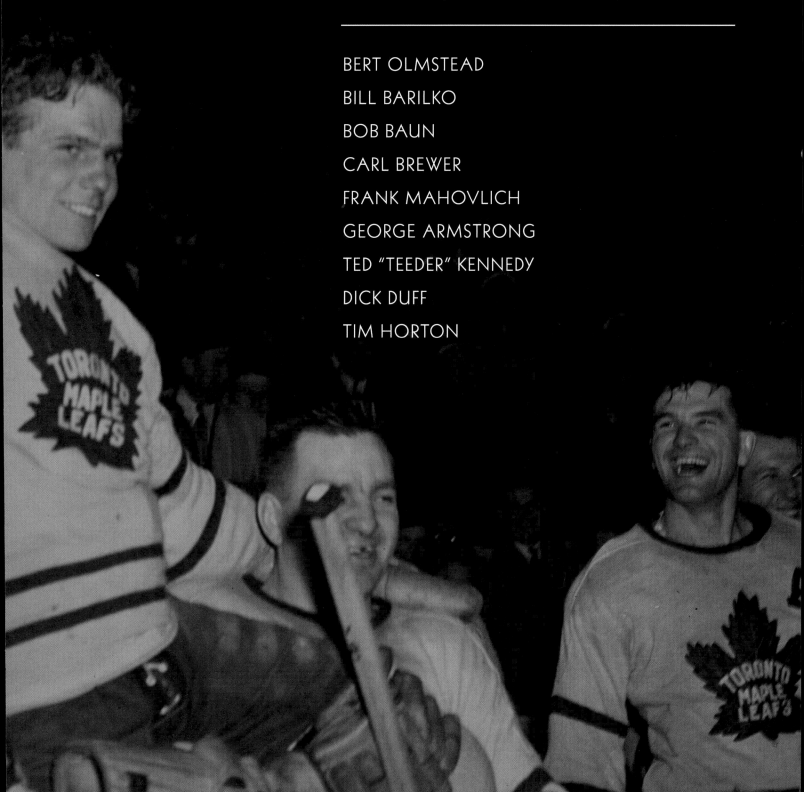

THE **1950**s

BERT OLMSTEAD

BILL BARILKO

BOB BAUN

CARL BREWER

FRANK MAHOVLICH

GEORGE ARMSTRONG

TED "TEEDER" KENNEDY

DICK DUFF

TIM HORTON

TEAM OF THE DECADE
1950–51 TORONTO MAPLE LEAFS, STANLEY CUP CHAMPIONS

REGULAR SEASON RECORD: 41-16-13

PLAYOFF RECORD: 8-2-1

In any other season, a five-game final against the Montreal Canadiens in which every game went into overtime would have emerged as the dominant storyline. However, Bill Barilko's tragic narrative trumped even that.

The Leafs used Al Rollins extensively in goal, and he played nine more games than Turk Broda and won the Vezina Trophy. But Broda's big-game pedigree won him the crease in the post-season. At 36, Broda continued his playoff mastery with a 1.10 goals against average and two shutouts. His final Cup would be his fifth, more than any other Toronto goalie.

Barilko became the first defenceman to score a Stanley Cup overtime winner. (It would take 19 more years for Bobby Orr to become the second.) The series ended at 2:53 in the first overtime when Barilko, poaching in the Montreal zone, sprang on a loose puck and lifted a shot past Montreal goalie Gerry McNeil. He would vanish without a trace a few months later in an airplane crash, and the image of an airborne Barilko scoring his famous goal would symbolize both success and tragedy.

16 BERT OLMSTEAD

  LEFT WING • 1958–59 TO 1961–62

Born: **September 7, 1926, Sceptre, Saskatchewan**
Games: **246** Goals: **56** Assists: **109** Points: **165** PIMs: **231**
Stanley Cup: **1962**
Inducted into Hockey Hall of Fame: **1985**

Bert Olmstead (right) and Jean Beliveau, November 15, 1955, Maple Leaf Gardens. The two players are one-two in leading the NHL in scoring

W hen he reached Toronto, Bert Olmstead was a light-scoring 32-year-old winger whose negligible statistical presence obscured his future contributions to the Leafs. Unrelenting in his drive for on-ice excellence, Olmstead was a powerful figure and one of the central architects of the Leafs' four Stanley Cup successes in the 1960s, even if he was only present for one.

A young Pat Quinn quickly grasped the standing Olmstead held in the dressing room. "Bert was a very committed, very solid player who didn't mind taking players to task if they weren't doing the things the team needed them to do," Quinn said. "He was a real leader and you can see it in how many times he played on Cup winners."

The game, Bert Olmstead said, had to be played correctly and it had to be played well, and woe to the teammate whose effort or thought process fell short.

"Bert was the best I ever heard in the room," said defenceman Larry Regan. "You might not want to repeat what he said in front of other people, but he was effective."

Bert Olmstead (left) and Pierre Pilote

Olmstead's status was so entrenched with management that when coach Punch Imlach was away from the team, Olmstead would run practice.

"He was very cantankerous," George Armstrong said. "We had a lot of young guys, they learned from him how to be a little cantankerous. When they made a mistake, he jumped on them. A lot of them didn't like it, but it was good for them. It caught on, a lot of people started giving each other hell and that's a good thing," Armstrong said.

Jacques Plante, who played with Olmstead in Montreal, marvelled at the will of the five-time Cup winner. "Bert Olmstead wasn't a very good skater," Plante said. "He wasn't stylish. All he could do was win."

BILL BARILKO

5

🏒 DEFENCE • 1946–47/1950–51

Born: **March 25, 1927, Timmins, Ontario** Died: **August 26, 1951 (24), Cochrane, Ontario**
Games: **252** Goals: **26** Assists: **36** Points: **62** PIMs: **456**
Stanley Cups: **1947, 1948, 1949, 1951**

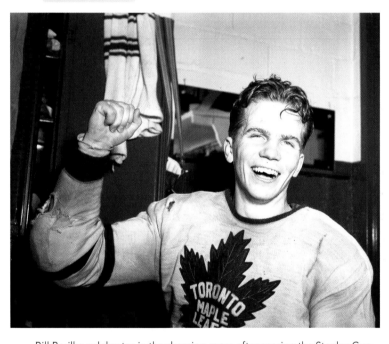

Bill Barilko celebrates in the dressing room after scoring the Stanley Cup–winning overtime goal in Game 5, April 21, 1951

Immortalized in the Tragically Hip song "Fifty Mission Cap" and honoured with one of only two retired numbers in Maple Leafs history (Ace Bailey is the other), Bill Barilko and his story have long since passed into legend.

He was known as Bashin' Bill, one of the league's best bodycheckers and a freewheeling defenceman who loved to venture deep in the offensive zone: a habit that distressed Leafs coach and former Kid Line great Joe Primeau. His greatest moment came in the fifth game of the 1951 Final.

Before the game, Primeau told Barilko: "Bill, I'm going to get a big hook and I'm going to throw it out there when you're out of position and I'm going to hook you back to your spot."

In overtime, Barilko dashed into the Montreal end and lifted a shot past Canadiens goalie Gerry McNeil to end the game and land the Leafs their fourth Cup in five years.

After his winner, Barilko teased Primeau: "You didn't want a hook on me that time, did you, Coach?"

Bill Barilko (right) and Sid Smith

It would be Bill Barilko's last game. That summer he embarked on a fishing trip with a Timmins dentist named Henry Hudson. His mother, deeply superstitious, despaired of his decision to fly with Hudson to a remote location to fish on a Friday.

"When he left, Bill's mom refused to speak to him," Barilko's sister Anne Klisanich said in the excellent book *Barilko: Without a Trace*. When Bill went in to say goodbye, his mother faked sleep and did not answer her son. It was the first and only time she didn't speak to him as he was leaving or kiss him goodbye, something that would haunt her forever.

On the way back, Barilko and Hudson refuelled at Rupert's House, a tiny community on the coast of James Bay. The pontoon plane was overloaded, and in an effort to lighten it, the two left their tents, sleeping bags, and cooking utensils. But 150 pounds of fish remained in the plane's pontoons. The overloaded plane never arrived home.

Despite the biggest air search in Canadian history, Barilko and Hudson disappeared in the wilds of northern Ontario, and Barilko faded into legend. The Leafs kept his jersey, number 5, hanging in the dressing room for the following season. Barilko was only 24 at the time of his death.

In June of 1962, 11 years after his disappearance, the wreck of the downed airplane was noticed by a bush pilot who saw the bright yellow paint of the pontoons. Only a few months earlier, the Leafs had captured their first Cup since Barilko's death.

Barilko was finally laid to rest in Timmins, his tombstone bearing his all-too-short lifespan, 1927 to 1951, and the four years he had won the Stanley Cup as a Leaf.

BOB BAUN

21

DEFENCE • 1956–57 TO 1966–67/1970–71 TO 1972–73

Born: **September 9, 1936, Lanigan, Saskatchewan**
Games: **739** Goals: **29** Assists: **140** Points: **169** PIMs: **1,155**
Stanley Cups: **1962, 1963, 1964, 1967**

Bob Baun hugging the Stanley Cup after the 1963 Maple Leafs win

Bob Baun was a rock-hard five-foot-nine defenceman, mined from the outdoor rinks of Saskatchewan. Baun, like Brian Glennie, practised the hip check, and he thrived for years as the defensive-minded partner for the offensively oriented Carl Brewer.

He was one of Conn Smythe's favourite players, a performer with perseverance and whose courage was forever cemented when he scored an overtime goal in the 1964 Stanley Cup playoffs while playing on a broken leg. His most gruesome injury happened in New York when an opposing player lost his balance and drove his skate blade into Baun's throat.

"The in-house doctor put some stitches in and said I was fine to go back out, but I wasn't feeling too well," Baun remembered. "I was sitting on the bus, and the players usually would dash down to a pub on 49th Street to grab a beer. For some reason, Tim Horton came back early and found me."

Baun had begun to hemorrhage. He does not remember how he got outside the bus and was unconscious when Horton threw him on his shoulder and ran him to a hospital down the block. It took emergency surgery and eight pints of blood to save him. A few days later, he flew from New York to a Toronto hospital and took a bed near his wife, who was about to deliver the couple's third son.

Bob Baun behind goaltender Terry Sawchuk with Jean Beliveau in hot pursuit

A cultured man who enjoyed good wine and fine dining, Bobby Baun was one of the few players versed in the business side of the game and often advised players in an era that preceded player agents. It was Baun, traded to Detroit, who told Gordie Howe that he had been radically underpaid and, in doing so, created a lasting rift between Howe and the Wings.

Baun played through countless injuries and spent 17 seasons in the NHL, 13 with the Leafs, until a neck injury finally induced him to end his career at 37. From his first game to his last, his courage, competitiveness, and willingness to endure pain to play overcame his skating and size.

"What you remember about Bobby Baun is his team play," said George Armstrong. "The team was number one. Even if something wasn't good for him, the team came first."

CARL
BREWER

♟ DEFENCE • 1957–58 TO 1964–65

Born: **October 21, 1938**, Toronto, Ontario Died: **August 25, 2001 (62)**, Toronto, Ontario
Games: **473** Goals: **19** Assists: **136** Points: **155** PIMs: **917**
Stanley Cups: **1962, 1963, 1964**

There is no legacy as mixed as the one left by Carl Brewer, a gifted puckhandling defenceman who teamed with Bobby Baun, won three Cups for the Leafs, and was a first-team all-star in 1963.

Brewer was a serial retiree. He retired after the 1959–60 season and told the media he was going to play football for McMaster University in Hamilton, where he was taking courses. The Leafs paid the bill and Brewer unretired.

Brewer sat out for four years after a training camp spat in 1965. During that time he regained his amateur standing, played for the Canadian National Team, anchored an International League team in Muskegon, Michigan, and then accepted an invitation to be a player coach in Finland with HIFK Helsinki. The first foreign-born star in the league, Brewer played and coached the club to the league title and thus became one of the Finnish sport's founding fathers.

It was a Brewer prerogative to change his mind. He feuded with Leafs GM Punch Imlach by insisting he be represented by agent Alan Eagleson. Thirty years later,

Carl Brewer skates past Bill Gadsby of the New York Rangers (Bob Pulford in background)

it would be Brewer who worked tirelessly to see that Eagleson was sent to prison for racketeering, fraud, and embezzlement.

Brewer re-entered the NHL to play with Detroit and St. Louis. He retired again but came back for a season in the WHA, quit for five years, and then made the most headshaking move in a career full of them. At the age of 41, he agreed to return to the Leafs blueline at the request of his old nemesis, Imlach. Brewer played 20 games and finished out the 79–80 season. "I guess," he said, "I've always had it on my mind to die a Maple Leaf."

Carl Brewer is in the Finnish Hockey Hall of Fame, number 147, between Gustav Bubnik and Curt Lindstrom. Leafs great Frank Mahovlich always felt Brewer deserved a spot in more than one Hall of Fame. "He was a brilliant hockey player," said the Big M. "He should have been in the Hockey Hall of Fame. He had so much talent."

A lion among the Leafs, Brewer died in August 2001 at the age of 62.

Mahovlich referring to his four-goal game

FRANK MAHOVLICH

LEFT WING • 1956–57 TO 1967–68

Born: **January 10, 1938, Timmins, Ontario**
Games: **720** Goals: **296** Assists: **301** Points: **597** PIMs: **782**
Stanley Cups: **1962, 1963, 1964, 1967**
Awards: **Calder Trophy, 1958**
Inducted into Hockey Hall of Fame: **1981**

If Frank Mahovlich wasn't the most talented Maple Leaf, and there are many who will argue that he was, he was certainly the most impressive to watch. Nothing could match the spectacle of Mahovlich picking the puck up in his end and roaring up the ice with long, powerful strides.

"On a given night, Frank Mahovlich was the greatest player that ever played," Bobby Hull once said.

"No one scores greater goals than Frank," said Dave Keon.

King Clancy, a fixture around the Gardens for 50 years, called him "Moses."

Mahovlich made goalscoring seem easy. In 1961, Mahovlich scored 43 goals in 56 games and seemed destined to break the vaunted 50 mark, but he went goal-less over the last 14 games. The drive for 50 turned into an ordeal, and Mahovlich never scored more than 36 as a Leaf again.

While Mahovlich scored 296 goals in blue and white, media, team-mates, and coaches always insisted there was room for more.

"Frank was so big, so skilled," said his teammate Pat Quinn. "There are some players who have so much skill it always feels they have more to give. I know that used to drive Punch crazy, but Frank was an amazing talent."

"Hockey is a streetcar named desire," Imlach once remarked, "and sometimes Frank doesn't catch it."

The Mahovlich-Imlach relationship was tragedy cast in broad strokes.

From left: Punch Imlach, Frank Mahovlich, and George Armstrong hold the big M's 100th goal puck, January 25, 1961

Imlach bought praise by the ounce. Perhaps more than any other Leaf, Mahovlich – an intelligent, sensitive man – struggled under the weight of Imlach's intensity.

The son of a hard-rock miner from Timmins, Ontario, Mahovlich found out that even when you realize your dreams, the challenges of life continue unabated. "Hockey is different than the vision I had as a kid," he once said. "Then, I thought if I ever got to the NHL, it would be the answer to life. I found out it isn't. I enjoy hockey, it's a satisfying job when things are right but some nights it's frustrating."

"Frank would have liked to have played the game with nobody knowing it," said his longtime teammate George Armstrong. "Playing the game was great, but the notoriety, walking down the street, people talking to him – that bothered him. Some of us love it, like Bobby Hull, but not Frank."

A trade to Detroit reinvigorated Mahovlich, and at 31 and 32, he turned in 49- and 38-goal seasons respectively. A sojourn in Montreal brought four more Cups. His 14 playoff goals in 1971 were an NHL record and his playmaking skills were so pronounced, he led the Habs in assists for three straight seasons.

After hockey, Frank Mahovlich went on to become a Canadian senator. Always a towering figure, he developed the qualities of a statesman as well as a superstar.

GEORGE
ARMSTRONG

RIGHT WING • 1949–50 AND 1951–52 TO 1970–71
COACH • 1988–89

Born: **July 6, 1930, Bowlands Bay, Ontario**
Games (player): **1,187** Goals: **296** Assists: **417** Points: **713** PIMs: **721**
Games (coach): **47** Record: **17 W, 26 L, 4 T** Pts. %: **.404**
Stanley Cups: **1962, 1963, 1964, 1967**
Inducted into Hockey Hall of Fame: **1975**

George Armstrong is a Sudbury, Ontario, product. His father, Fred, was Irish and worked underground in the nickel mines for 40 years.

If the nickname "Chief" was given to George Armstrong as a nod to his First Nation roots (through his mother), it also spoke to his standing with every team he played for. The Leafs dressing room in the 1960s was often awash in determined personalities: from young, strong-willed players such as Bob Pulford, Carl Brewer, and Dave Keon to flinty veterans like Bert Olmstead and Terry Sawchuk. At the centre of the room was Chief: joker, counsellor, mentor, negotiator, liaison, and, for good measure, one of the best checking wingers in the league.

Armstrong played 1,187 games and scored 296 regular season goals. The men who played with him remember a stable of characters: Chief, Chiefy-Cat, Digger.

"He'd walk around the dressing room with no teeth in," longtime teammate Jim McKenny once said. "He looked like Popeye, except he had string bean arms, string bean legs, and a pot. He couldn't go by the full-length mirror without giving a flex. He always called himself 'Digger.' He'd say, 'Digger, you're beautiful.'"

George Armstrong with coach Punch Imlach

Armstrong was always the best dressing room mimic. When coach Punch Imlach would deliver blistering sermons, Armstrong would sometimes make faces behind his back.

The locker room cut-up was a prodigious notetaker who studied the game relentlessly to cement his place inside it. He was an expert in forcing opponents to bad ice, but typically, he undersold that talent.

"Playing good defence is easy," he once said. "If you do it right, the puck never comes to you."

His ungainly skating usually got him where he wanted to go.

"When he was going down the ice against a defenceman, it always looked like he was going to fall down," longtime teammate Allan Stanley once said, "but he always ended up on the other side of the defenceman with a good chance."

"I've read where people said he didn't have a lot of talent," said Hall of Fame goalie Glenn Hall. "I've never agreed with that. He was an excellent player who was very dangerous in front of the net."

"He was so strong in the corner," said Johnny Bower, Armstrong's longtime roommate and dressing-room foil. "When he crossed his stick over the other guy's stick, there was no way the other player could move."

A four-time Cup winner, Armstrong is remembered by fans for scoring the empty-net goal that climaxed the 1967 Stanley Cup win over Montreal. He is remembered by the men in the dressing room for the leadership that powered the Leafs.

TED "TEEDER" KENNEDY

CENTRE • 1942–43 TO 1956–57

Born: **December 12, 1925, Humberstone, Ontario** Died: **August 14, 2009 (83), Port Colborne, Ontario**
Games: **696** Goals: **231** Assists: **329** Points: **560** PIMs: **432**
Stanley Cups: **1945, 1947, 1948, 1949, 1951**
Awards: **Hart Trophy, 1955**
Inducted into Hockey Hall of Fame: **1966**

Conn Smythe kept his own exclusive Hall of Fame. There was in his office only one framed picture of a player. It was of Ted "Teeder" Kennedy.

"Ted Kennedy was number one," Smythe once explained, "because he was a brilliant leader. He'd played on five world championship teams before he was 26."

Ted Kennedy was the product of his times and his background. He was the fourth and final child in a working class family in what is now Port Colborne, Ontario. A month before his birth, his father, Gordon Kennedy, was killed in a hunting accident and Ted was born to a grieving mother.

Margaret Kennedy now needed a second income. She took a job selling snacks at a neighbouring arena. She brought Ted to work with her, and he learned the work ethic that defined him literally at the feet of his mother.

A captain at 22, Kennedy led his team to five Stanley Cups and, in recognition of his sterling career, he won the Hart Trophy in 1955.

Ted Kennedy with his wife and son, May 5, 1955. Kennedy holds his milestone 200 regular season NHL goal stick

"With a guy like Teeder, it was born into him," said Sid Smith, a Kennedy linemate for six seasons. "He wanted to be good all the time and he wanted you to be good all the time."

"All the players looked up to Teeder," said forward Bob Davidson. "They just had to look at the expression on his face when he went into the faceoff circle. He was so intense."

Kennedy was also a fan favourite, particularly with his #1 fan, John Arnott. Arnott was a Torontonian with a deep devotion for the Leafs and a Gardens regular during the 1940s and 1950s. In the days when an organ was the only musical accompaniment to a game, Arnott's booming shout of "Come on, Teeder!" from the blue seats was as much a part of the night's game as popcorn. Arnott was such a devout fan, the team granted him occasional access to the dressing room and saved him a spot in a car during at least one Stanley Cup parade. Later in life, the two met up again and became great friends. When John Arnott died in 1980 at the age of 81, Ted Kennedy was one of his pallbearers.

"For me, it was a dream come true to play in the National Hockey League," Kennedy once said. "Being a captain, being inducted into the Hall of Fame, as honourable as those might be, it was incidental really. It wasn't something I set out to do. All I wanted was the opportunity to prove myself against my peers."

DICK
DUFF

 LEFT WING • 1954–55 TO 1963–64

Born: **February 18, 1936, Kirkland Lake, Ontario**
Games: **582** Goals: **174** Assists: **168** Points: **339** PIMs: **535**
Stanley Cups: **1962, 1963**
Inducted into Hockey Hall of Fame: **2006**

Dick Duff (right) and Bob Nevin celebrate following Game 6 of the Stanley Cup final, April 22, 1962, Chicago Stadium. Toronto Beat Chicago 2–1

D ick Duff was many things: a teen idol, clutch performer, and one of the Leafs' most diligent, hard-working players. Mined, like so many others, from northern Ontario, Duff was tutored in the Maple Leafs way through the St. Mike's hockey development system.

"The Toronto Maple Leafs had two principal advantages over the competition," veteran hockey writer Frank Orr once observed. "Foster Hewitt's broadcasts and the Basilian Fathers of St. Mike's School."

Duff was just 18 when he stepped into a Leafs uniform. His listed height of five foot nine flew in the face of the Brothers' observance of the ninth commandment: thou shalt not lie.

In his first full season, Duff scored 18 goals. He would record 26- and 29-goal campaigns and establish himself as a fierce player, more than happy to pester his check off the scoresheet.

Duff had an envious habit of scoring big goals. When the Leafs nailed down the playoff spot in 1959, Duff scored twice in the final regular season game to

Dick Duff scores on goalie Charlie Hodge

get them there. He scored an overtime winner in the Final, but the Leafs lost to Montreal in five games. Duff scored the Stanley Cup–wining goal in 1962 as the Leafs eliminated the Chicago Black Hawks, and in the 1963 Final against Detroit, he opened the series with two goals in the first 1:08. The Leafs captured the Stanley Cup in six games.

Duff relished his role as a big-time, big-game player. "I was fired up if the score was tied or one goal apart," he once said. "The playoffs are the real test of desire and skill."

Duff parlayed his strong work ethic and desire to win into seven all-star appearances and a lasting place in the Hockey Hall of Fame as an honoured member in 2006.

7

TIM
HORTON

 DEFENCE • 1949–50/1951–52 TO 1969–70

Born: **January 12, 1930, Cochrane, Ontario** Died: **February 21, 1974 (44), St. Catharines, Ontario**
Games: **1,185** Goals: **109** Assists: **349** Points: **458** PIMs: **1,389**
Stanley Cups: **1962, 1963, 1964, 1967**
Inducted into Hockey Hall of Fame: **1977**

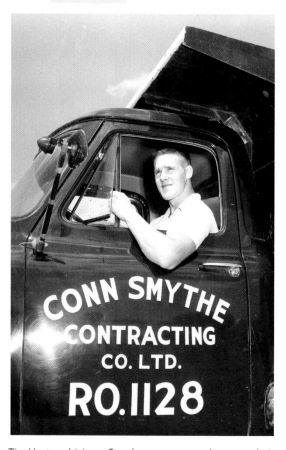

Tim Horton driving a Smythe company truck at a sand pit

Tim Horton played an astonishing 24 seasons in the NHL and is widely recognized as the strongest man who played in the league during his time. He was also known as the most gentle; Horton rarely fought, largely out of a disdain for hurting his opponent. In Horton's final season, he was challenged by Philadelphia Flyers tough guy Dave Schultz. Rather than pummel Schultz, Horton bearhugged him and sat on him as both benches roared with laughter.

Horton was a wild extrovert who loved a good time. "When Tim pounded on your hotel room door, you got out of bed like a shot," said Paul Henderson. "If you didn't get to the door fast enough, he'd just put his shoulder into it and bust through it and then you'd be on the hook for the repair job."

There is no record for the number of players he helped shepherd through the league or the countless acts of kindness he extended toward those who played with him. Generous, open-hearted, and brave, he was beloved by those who played with him. Said his longtime teammate George Armstrong, "There was no finer teammate, no finer man than Tim Horton."

Horton's eyesight was so poor that he struggled to hit the net. He played 486 straight games, a Maple Leafs record. He was the first Leaf to reach the 1,000-game mark.

Beneath the soft exterior lay a fearless competitor.

Tim Horton battles past Bob Nevin of the New York Rangers

"I remember warning Tim Horton about a player who was tough in the corners who would try to intimidate him," Conn Smythe once said. "He said, 'Mr. Smythe, I'm not afraid of no man living.'"

Horton was killed in a traffic accident in 1974 just as the restaurant chain he founded was beginning to pick up momentum. Many mourned the loss of this beloved man. Every Leaf, regardless of rank, had a friend in Tim Horton.

Celebrating the end of Game 5 of the Stanley Cup final, 1963

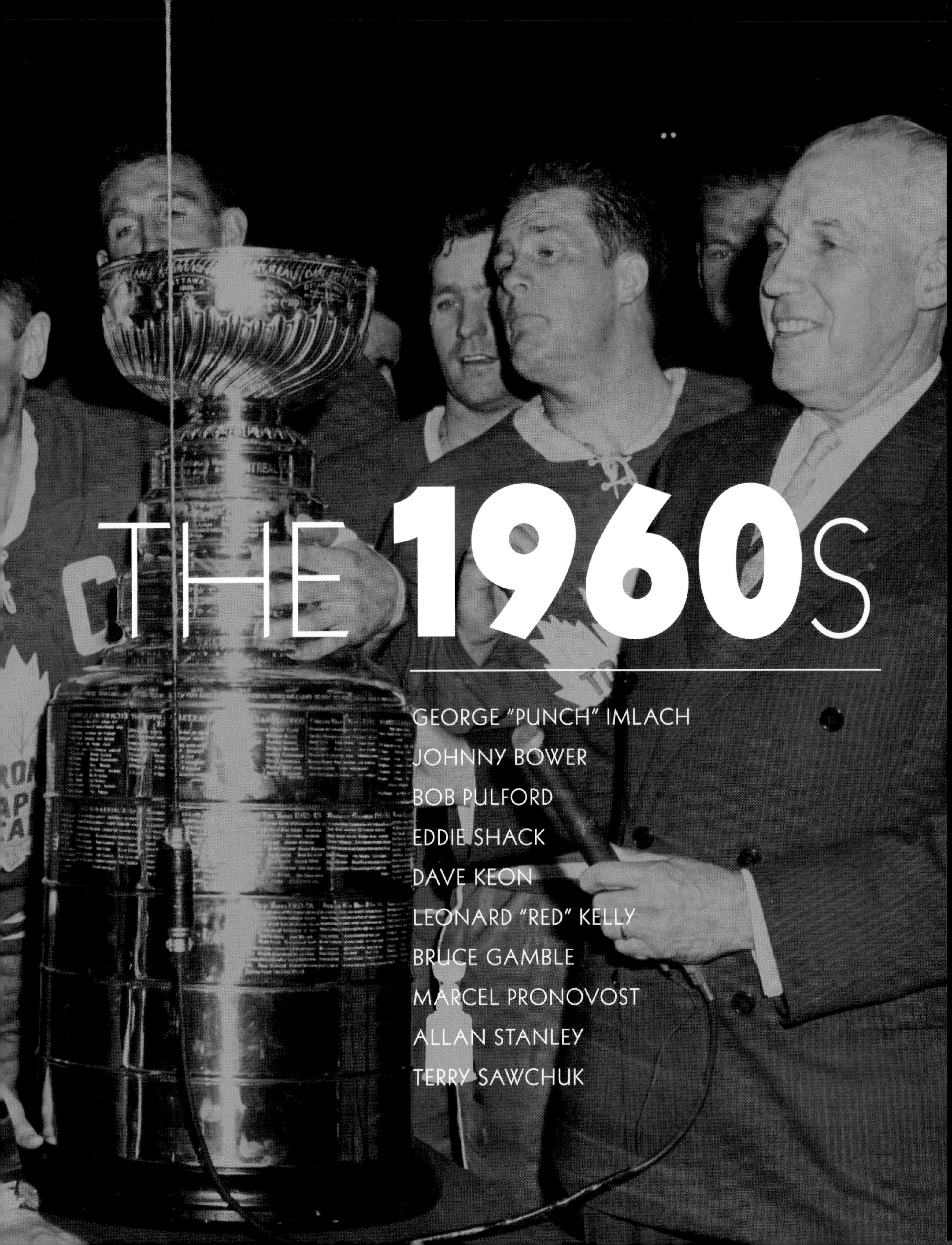

THE 1960s

GEORGE "PUNCH" IMLACH

JOHNNY BOWER

BOB PULFORD

EDDIE SHACK

DAVE KEON

LEONARD "RED" KELLY

BRUCE GAMBLE

MARCEL PRONOVOST

ALLAN STANLEY

TERRY SAWCHUK

TEAM OF THE DECADE
1962–63 TORONTO MAPLE LEAFS, STANLEY CUP CHAMPIONS

REGULAR SEASON RECORD: 33-22-11
PLAYOFF RECORD: 8-4

Dave Keon considers the 1963 Cup–winning team "the best team I ever played for and the best in the history of the team. We were never that good again," he said.

The Leafs were the class of the league all season. Their longest losing streak was three games and it happened once. The club lost only two of its last 12 games. They finished in first place and then cruised to the Stanley Cup, winning eight of 12 games.

The roster was replete with impact players coming into their primes. Twenty-six-year-old Frank Mahovlich scored 36 goals, his second-highest total as a Leaf. Just 22, Keon was asserting himself as one of the great talents in the game on the strength of a 28-goal, 56-point season and superb two-way play. Bob Pulford was 26 and in the top handful of defensive forwards. Twenty-six-year-old Dick Duff, a 16-goal-scorer in the regular season potted two goals in the first 1:08 of Game 1. Five separate players – Duff, Bob Nevin, Ron Stewart, Red Kelly, and Keon – scored two goals in a game, and two of Keon's team-leading seven playoff goals were short-handed.

Bower, a relatively spry 36, played every minute and delivered a playoff-best 1.60 goals against average. Every position player who played more than one game netted a post-season point and 12 of the 18 scored at least one goal. Counting Tim Horton, Frank Mahovlich, and Johnny Bower, half of the 1963 Maple Leafs were Hall of Fame bound.

The Leafs swept all six of their home playoff games, outscoring Montreal 11–3 in games at the Gardens. The Red Wings fared little better; the Leafs outscored Detroit 11–5 in Toronto.

GEORGE "PUNCH" IMLACH

  COACH • 1959–68/1979–80

Born: **March 15, 1918, Toronto, Ontario** Died: **December 1, 1987 (69), Toronto, Ontario**
Games: **760** Record: **370 W, 272 L, 125 T** Pts. %: **.562**
Stanley Cups: **1962, 1963, 1964, 1967**
Inducted into Hockey Hall of Fame: **1984 (Builder)**

They called George Imlach "Punch" because as an undistinguished young hockey player he was knocked woozy by an elbow and in his stupor took a number of swings at the trainer who had come to tend to him. The nickname was perfect. Punch Imlach was a fighter who became one of the most successful coaches in the club's history. His teams made the playoffs in 10 of his 11 years as coach, GM, or both. He won four Stanley Cups, second only to Hap Day, who won five.

An only child born into a working-class Toronto neighbourhood, Punch Imlach evolved into a towering figure, a skinflint coach/general manager who favoured understated but expensive suits, fine watches, and even the violin, which he played superbly as a boy. His trademark hats came free from the manufacturer.

His early ambition was to be an accountant. As a young man he worked as a bank clerk. Imlach drifted into coaching when handed the reins of the senior Quebec Aces. He was keeping the books for a Quebec City–based pulp and paper company at the time. He advanced to the NHL with a style built on confrontation. He believed in treating every player the same way: strictly.

"Sure, you can take a guy aside in a bus or a plane and tell him whatever you have to make him play better," he once said. "But in the locker room, you can't make exceptions. You've got to treat everybody the same.

If a guy is a sensitive type who can't take the harsh stuff, well, that's life. And if a guy tries to back me into a corner and challenge me, look out."

Imlach breathed life into the careers of players thought to be near the end of their time in the league. The 1967 Leafs were the oldest championship team in sports history. Despite some young legs, including 26-year-old Dave Keon and 22-year-old Ron Ellis, the roster was running on fumes. Eight players were 35 years or older. They were, in the words of their coach, the Old Fellows Athletic Club.

The team worked hard to pull off a miracle. They deployed five different goalies and, as of late February, had lost a record 10 games in a row. They made the play-offs on the final night of the post-season. But the goaltending settled when 43-year-old Johnny Bower and 38-year-old Terry Sawchuk managed to stay reasonably intact. Bower stopped 62 shots in one overtime playoff win against Montreal.

From left: Frank Mahovlich, Bob Pulford, Punch Imlach, and Bob Nevin

"Between us," Bower said in the wake of the victory, "we had enough working parts for one goalie."

"Some of you have been with me for nine years," Punch Imlach told the team before that final night. "It's been said that I stuck with the old guys so long we couldn't possibly win the Stanley Cup. For some of you, it's a farewell. Get out there and jam the puck down their throats."

Sawchuk, a four-time Cup winner, called it the most satisfying victory of his career. So did Kelly, who had won eight.

After he left Toronto, Imlach resurfaced in Buffalo as a GM. Harold Ballard then brought him back in 1979 for two tumultuous years.

There is no denying Imlach's contribution to Maple Leafs history. While his players often intimated they performed for themselves and in spite of their coach, it was also true they often played beyond their ability for Imlach.

"He had the touch," said Don Cherry, who knew Imlach during his days as a Leafs farmhand. "He could put confidence in players. He'd do anything to win. If you were in the way of him winning, you were gone. It was win at all costs."

He was bold and brash, and unconventional in many ways. Just before the 1967 Montreal win, he brought $2,000 in small bills, dumped it out in front of the players, and reminded them that one final win would bring that sum in bonus money.

Imlach was up front in his demands. He would often ask players if they would tolerate playing for him

Coach Punch Imlach in the dressing room at the conclusion of Game 6 of the Stanley Cup final, May 2, 1967

before they were acquired. The highest accolade he accorded his players was the ability to withstand their coach. "He played well for me" was for Imlach a glowing endorsement.

"I guess you're probably gonna call me a complex guy and I guess I am," he once told an interviewer. "There's a lot of sides to me, but you know what they say, like me or hate me: there's no in between."

JOHNNY BOWER

GOALTENDER • 1958–59 TO 1969–70

Born: **November 8, 1924, Prince Albert, Saskatchewan**
Games: **472** Wins: **220** Losses: **161** Ties: **79** Shutouts: **33** Goals against: **2.51**
Stanley Cups: **1962, 1963, 1964, 1967**
Awards: **Vezina Trophy, 1961, 1965**
Inducted into Hockey Hall of Fame: **1976**

I t used to puzzle Johnny Bower when people said that because he spent 12 seasons in the minors, he spent much of his career in the wrong place at the wrong time.

As a young soldier in the Second World War, Bower's ill health kept him from what promised to be a particularly robust adventure. The destination was a port in France named Dieppe, and many of the boys Bower chummed with never came home.

At 33, Johnny Bower found himself in the American League. He was comfortable there. Bower spent one season in the NHL as a New York Ranger, and the way he had been discarded when the Rangers' regular goalie, Gump Worsley, returned from injury had soured him on big-league life.

Then the Leafs called.

"I wasn't really interested in playing with the Leafs," he would say. "I was in a good situation in Cleveland, and I figured I would finish my career there."

The Leafs were being rebuilt under Punch Imlach, one of the rare NHL general managers who viewed advanced age in an athlete as a quality not a liability.

Johnny Bower in the Leafs dressing room during the 1959–60 season

Johnny Bower wearing the mask used in practice

Despite rheumatoid arthritis, a condition he endured all his life, Bower played 12 more seasons with the Leafs. He won the Vezina Trophy at 37 years of age and split another with Terry Sawchuk when he was 41. He played his final NHL game as a 45-year-old.

Bower approached every game, every practice, like it would be his last. He considered a goal allowed a personal affront. The Leafs lost many of Bower's goal sticks when he cracked them against the crossbar after surrendering a goal in practice.

His genial nature belied an unrelenting drive to succeed. "His desire to stop the puck was unbelievable," said his longtime roommate George Armstrong. "He had a thing, he never wanted a puck behind him in the net in practice. When we practised, we'd have about 100 pucks. We'd have to stop the practice because there would be 100 pucks in Sawchuk's net and none in Bower's."

Except for the very end of his career, Bower refused to wear a facemask because he felt it compromised his vision. His signature move, a sliding poke check, involved putting his face directly in the line of an opponent's churning skates.

His timing, it turns out, had always been picture perfect.

"When I got to Toronto, we had some terrific young players in Dave Keon and Frank Mahovlich and Punch got us some great veterans in Allan Stanley and Bert Olmstead," said the immortal Johnny Bower. "I got there at just the right time."

BOB PULFORD

 CENTRE, LEFT WING • 1956–57 TO 1969–70

Born: **March 31, 1936, Newton Robinson, Ontario**
Games: **947** Goals: **251** Assists: **312** Points: **563** PIMs: **691**
Stanley Cups: **1962, 1963, 1964, 1967**
Inducted into Hockey Hall of Fame: **1991**

Throughout his 14 seasons, Bob Pulford was a game-changer, a dogged two-way forward and consistent scorer who would become one of the Leafs' most accomplished and least recognized stars.

The plus-minus statistic had not yet been invented during Pulford's career, but opponents and teammates nonetheless recognized his abilities and his dedication to his craft.

"Pulford is what's known in the trade as a 'hockey player's hockey player,'" said Montreal Canadiens coach Toe Blake.

"Pulford is one of my private headaches because he has to be classed as one of hockey's greatest forecheckers," said Gordie Howe.

Punch Imlach gave Pulford the ultimate endorsement in 1967, the night the Leafs won their most recent Stanley Cup. With 55 seconds to play, Pulford was sent onto the ice along with Leafs veterans Red Kelly, Tim Horton, Allan Stanley, and George Armstrong. The Canadiens could not register a shot.

What he might have lacked in finesse, he made up in hard work. "I'm an average player," said Pulford. "I know I'm lacking as a skater. I plug more and work hard and get my share of goals. I think hard work can make up for a lot of things that a hockey player may lack."

A well-rounded person, Pulford attended classes at McMaster University in Hamilton, Ontario, three nights a week for six years to earn a degree, but

From left: Bob Baun, Bob Pulford, and Gordie Howe during Game 6 of the Stanley Cup final series in Detroit, April 3, 1960

if his game was built on intelligence and hard work, it was often fuelled by anger. It was Pulford who initiated the change to the two penalty-box system. For years players from the two teams shared the penalty box with an often-nervous attendant or policeman sitting between them. One night in Toronto, Pulford became so furious at Montreal defenceman Terry Harper that he rushed at him in the box. The Leafs, mindful of losing one of their better players to suspension, walled off the two boxes for the rest of the game and the change stuck.

"He was an excellent player," said longtime captain George Armstrong, "but as good as he was, he was even better when he was angry. When someone would hit him hard, his face would get red. We'd see that on the bench and say to ourselves 'tonight we're really in business.'"

EDDIE
SHACK

RIGHT WING • 1960–61 TO 1966–67/1973–74 TO 1974–75

Born: **February 11, 1937, Sudbury, Ontario**
Games: **504** Goals: **99** Assists: **96** Points: **195** PIMs: **676**
Stanley Cups: **1962, 1963, 1964, 1967**

Eddie Shack played 504 games for the Leafs as a rabble-rouser whose good skating skills invariably landed him in trouble with opposition players and sometimes his own teammates.

Adoring fans, and they were legion, called him "The Entertainer."

A four-time Cup winner, Shack was a burly six foot one and one of the few players who could match up physically with Gordie Howe. Shack, of course, was no Gordie Howe, but he did score the Cup-winning goal in 1963 and once potted 26 goals in a season.

It was said of Eddie Shack that he played all three forward positions at the same time. Canadian hockey writer Stephen Cole likened his playing to "a big puppy let loose in a wild field."

He invariably irritated whomever he was playing against and sometimes, to Shack's chagrin, his own teammates.

Once, veteran Bert Olmstead grabbed Shack by the shoulder pads between periods.

"Eddie," he said. "What colours am I wearing?"

"Blue and white," Shack replied.

"And what colours are you wearing?"

"Blue and white," came Shack's reply.

"So do you think you could stop running into me," said Olmstead. "We're on the same team."

Shack often disrupted practice with wild head-high shots on Terry Sawchuk. "As soon as Shackie sent a shot past Terry's ears, that would be it," said defenceman Bob Baun. "Terry hated to practise, and after that he would skate around and go anywhere but into the net. Shackie was a great teammate, but sometimes you wondered if it would be easier to be playing against him than with him."

Shack was a hustler long before he reached Toronto. He began working in his hometown of Sudbury, Ontario, delivering meat for a butcher when he was eight years old. By his 10th birthday, he had his own stand at the farmer's market. When the carnival came through, he worked for them too. Shack would make himself one of the most affluent Leafs of his era with holdings in golf courses and a steady stream of endorsements.

"I don't know what I've got, but it's something the crowd likes," The Entertainer once said. "When I'm walking to the press box and it's announced I'm not going to play, I hear the crowd sort of sigh."

Eddie Shack yells at Gump Worsley while trying to score

DAVE
KEON

C CENTRE • 1960–61 TO 1974–75

Born: **March 22, 1940, Rouyn-Noranda, Quebec**
Games: **1,062** Goals: **365** Assists: **493** Points: **858** PIMs: **75**
Stanley Cups: **1962, 1963, 1964, 1967**
Awards: **Calder Trophy, 1962; Lady Byng Trophy, 1962, 1963; Conn Smythe Trophy, 1967**
Inducted into Hockey Hall of Fame: **1986**

Dave Keon in the foreground sitting beside Marcel Pronovost

Dave Keon was from the mining town of Rouyn-Noranda, Quebec. His father, David, was a miner who never complained about a life built on toil. His mother, Laura, was a brilliant school teacher. Keon built his game on those twin poles: a Spartan work ethic shaped by a sharp intelligence.

Only five foot nine and 165 pounds, little Davey Keon was a superb skater who understood the game's geometry better than nearly any player of his era. He went into the corners recklessly, finished his checks efficiently, and dominated the faceoff circle. He hit the 20-goal mark 11 times in his 15 Leafs seasons and three times bettered 30. The wonder of Dave Keon, and there were many, is how one of the most driven, competitive of Maple Leafs only accrued 75 penalty minutes in 1,062 games as a Leaf.

It is a testimony to Keon's iron will that the skill that originally delayed his Leafs debut as a 19-year-old freshman was a weak defensive game.

"I got a message a year before I played with the Leafs when they didn't bring me up," Keon said. "I improved

Dave Keon with his son

Dave Keon puts a backhand past Glenn Hall

my checking that last season at St. Mike's because I realized that's what had to be done."

Keon brought a veteran's sense to his rookie year. He learned how to position himself squarely in front of his check and to stop instead of turning away when his check stopped skating. He scored 20 goals, banked 45 points, and won the Calder Trophy in his rookie season. In his second, he scored 26 goals and finished with 61 points and earned only one minor penalty.

For most of his career, he drew the opposition's best players.

"I can only tell you about Jean Beliveau, Stan Mikita, Alex Delvecchio, and whoever the real good centres of the day were," Keon once said. "Those are the only guys I saw."

LEONARD "RED"
KELLY

CENTRE • 1959–60 TO 1966–67
COACH • 1973–77

Born: **July 9, 1927, Simcoe, Ontario**
Games (player): **470** Goals: **119** Assists: **232** Points: **351** PIMs: **74**
Games (coach): **318** Record: **133 W, 123 L, 62 T** Pts. %: **.516**
Stanley Cups: **1962, 1963, 1964, 1967**
Awards: **Lady Byng Trophy, 1961**
Inducted into Hockey Hall of Fame: **1969**

From a frozen pond on his family's tobacco farm in Simcoe, Ontario, Leonard "Red" Kelly went on to win eight Stanley Cups – four as a wheelhouse defenceman for the Detroit Red Wings and four more as a centreman with the Leafs. While he left the farm, it never quite left him, and his work ethic and quiet nature spoke to his early life.

Kelly might not have been naturally talented, but he made himself into a player. As a kid, he was considered a longshot to make the St. Michael's juniors. A Detroit scout only signed him because the Boston Bruins had inked a number of players off that St. Mike's team and he didn't want his bosses to think he wasn't paying attention.

It was easy to mistake Kelly's soft demeanour for a lack of fire.

Leafs scout Squib Walker bet a colleague that Kelly's gentle nature would limit his NHL career to less

Red Kelly hugs the Stanley Cup in 1963

Red Kelly signs autographs

than 20 games. Kelly played 20 years. Kelly had been a lightweight boxing champ in his undergraduate days, and when provoked, he was a devastating fighter. Everyone in the six-team league understood the dire repercussions of underestimating Red Kelly.

Kelly worked tirelessly to make himself a better skater and quickly developed a knack for understanding and influencing the rhythms of a game. He was sure-handed in his own end and exceptionally creative in the attack. He led NHL defencemen in goals eight times.

In February 1960, Kelly angered Detroit GM Jack Adams by telling a newspaperman he had played in the previous playoff at management's encouragement despite a badly injured ankle. The tyrannical Adams hated bad publicity and quickly traded Kelly to the New York Rangers. Once again, Kelly's resolve had been underestimated. Kelly stunned Adams and the league establishment when he said he would retire rather than report to New York. Despite the admonishment of NHL president Clarence Campbell, Kelly would not be budged. He resented the impunity with which Adams had acted and was offended by stories subsequently planted in the Detroit media that he was slowing down at age 32.

Leafs GM Punch Imlach rightly reckoned Kelly could be had at a bargain price and landed him in exchange for a journeyman named Marc Reaume. "Jack Adams gave my wife away six months before. Then he gave me away," Kelly later joked.

Out of playing shape because of the layoff, Kelly volunteered to ease into the Leafs lineup as a centre.

"I haven't been on skates for 10 days. Maybe I should play up front where a couple of goofs won't quite be as costly," Kelly told Leafs coach Punch Imlach.

"Not a bad idea," Imlach said. "We're playing the Canadiens tomorrow night and you can check Beliveau."

Kelly never went back to the blueline and reeled off seasons of 20, 22, and 20 goals in his new position.

Immensely popular, Kelly was urged by Prime Minister Lester Pearson to run as a Member of Parliament while still a player. Kelly won two terms, flew to Ottawa weekly, and never missed a game. Kelly's maiden speech in the House of Commons was in support of the new Canadian flag. The flag debate was a source of lengthy conversations between Kelly and Conn Smythe, who favoured the Red Ensign. History, as it usually did, would prove Red Kelly right.

As a coach, Kelly was popular and known for his willingness to try anything that worked. In the 1976 Cup series, Red Kelly was looking for a gimmick. Not only were the Leafs heavy underdogs against the powerhouse

Red Kelly (right) and Frank Mahovlich after Game 3 of the Stanley Cup semi-final series on March 27, 1960, in Detroit. Toronto beat Detroit 5–4 in triple overtime; Mahovlich scored the winner assisted by Kelly

Philadelphia Flyers, they were up against a good-luck charm whose presence revved up the Spectrum crowd and contributed to a lopsided home-ice advantage. Kate Smith's recording of "God Bless America" threw fans into a frenzy. So Kelly hit upon the mystical power of the great pyramids.

Kelly installed small pyramids under the Leafs bench, hoping their mystical qualities would translate into on-ice success. It worked … for a time. Darryl Sittler, mired in a playoff-long slump, scored five times in the Leafs' 8–5 home-ice win.

The gimmick had the double advantage of funnelling the media toward Kelly and away from the players. "We needed something to take the players' minds off what was going on in town," he said.

Before Game 7, Kelly had the Leafs sit under a giant pyramid in the visitors' dressing room. Cracked Tiger Williams: "Thank God I don't play for Philadelphia. I would have to sit under Kate Smith."

Pyramid power ran out of steam in Game 7 as the Flyers triumphed 7–3.

"If you think something can happen – if the players believe it – then that's great," Kelly said. "That's what I was trying to do, get them all thinking the right way. And they almost pulled it off."

BRUCE GAMBLE

GOALTENDER • 1965–66 TO 1970–71

Born: **May 24, 1938**, Port Arthur, Ontario Died: **December 29, 1982 (44)**, Niagara Falls, Ontario
Games: **210** Wins: **82** Losses: **83** Ties: **31** Shutouts: **19** Goals against: **2.94**

From the beginning, Bruce Gamble did things his way. As a Leaf, Gamble was one of the last holdouts to the facemask. When he finally consented in 1970, the list of bare-faced goalies went from four to three.

Gamble's courage was evident to his teammates. "I never saw a guy with more guts or more desire to play," Johnny Bower once said. "He'd go when he had the flu when he should have been in bed. Boy, he had the desire."

Gamble played 10 years with Toronto, Boston, and the Flyers. He suffered a heart attack while tending goal for the Flyers in a game in 1972. He actually played through the attack; only the next day was his condition diagnosed. A doctor's pronouncement that he must never play again ended Gamble's goaltending career. To risk any excessive exercise, the experts said, was to court death. He was 34.

Gamble scouted a year for the Flyers and then disappeared.

His reclusiveness went from puzzling to newsworthy. Hockey people searched for his location so that he could be forwarded the paperwork on his pension. The *Toronto Sun* ran a photo of Gamble as a Leaf with the headline: "Have you seen this man?"

Gamble's location was unknown for a decade. There were rumours he was in one city operating an ice-cream truck or working construction. Few knew the truth: Gamble had been living quietly by himself in Niagara Falls, Ontario.

From left: Bobby Orr and Bruce Gamble during the 1968–69 season

Even if the NHL was forever out of reach, the pull of the game never let go of Bruce Gamble. The night before his death, Gamble had been practising with an oldtimers hockey team in Niagara Falls. He went to the hospital the next morning with chest pain. The heart attack foretold by the doctors took Bruce Gamble at 44.

Johnny Bower was never more right. He just had the desire.

MARCEL PRONOVOST

 DEFENCE • 1965–66 TO 1969–70

Born: **June 15, 1930, Lac-à-la-Tortue, Quebec**
Games: **223** Goals: **8** Assists: **40** Points: **48** PIMs: **134**
Stanley Cup: **1967**
Inducted into Hockey Hall of Fame: **1978**

Maybe it was his background – he was raised in a tiny Quebec town as 1 of 12 children, nine boys, who took to the ice in shifts to trade off their skates – but Marcel Pronovost never took a shift off as an NHL player.

The Hall of Fame defenceman was one of the architects of the Leafs' 1967 Stanley Cup win, an imposing shutdown defender whose game was based on courage and smarts. He was also a prodigious winner, a man whose passionate game and explosive power to hit made him a five-time champion and a performer in 11 all-star games. It was said that no one played through as many injuries as Marcel Pronovost. He once estimated that his nose had been broken at least a dozen times.

In 1965, after 15 seasons in Detroit, Pronovost was acquired by the Leafs and added five years more in Toronto. Pronovost was on the ice for just two goals against in the 1967 playoffs as the Leafs upended powerhouse Chicago and Montreal.

"He was a great player," said his coach, Punch Imlach. "He and [Montreal's star defenceman] Doug Harvey were the two best defencemen in the league for some time and Marcel was always durable. How else do you explain 1,200 games in the league?"

"I was not one of the better players, but I was one of the hardest-working players," Pronovost once said. "I wasn't afraid of anything and gave the game everything I had."

Marcel Provonost (left) and Dave Keon in the dressing room celebrating after Game 6 of the Stanley Cup final in Toronto, May 2, 1967

ALLAN STANLEY

 DEFENCE • 1958–59 TO 1967–68

Born: **March 1, 1926, Timmins, Ontario** Died: **October 18, 2013 (87), Bobcaygeon, Ontario**
Games: **633** Goals: **47** Assists: **186** Points: **233** PIMs: **318**
Stanley Cups: **1962, 1963, 1964, 1967**
Inducted into Hockey Hall of Fame: **1981**

Allan Stanley was so quiet his teammates dubbed him "Silent Sam." Stanley was also one of the most intelligent, instinctive players in franchise history.

Three times a second-team all-star, Stanley was usually overlooked as all eyes naturally followed his defence partner, Tim Horton. Stanley was 31 when he came to Toronto, and his arrival coincided with Horton's best seasons.

Horton, for one, disagreed with the idea that Stanley's value lay only in defending. "Everyone said I did the rushing and he played defence, but he had an uncanny sense of when the play would change from offence to defence and there were a lot of times he was leading the charge," Horton said.

No one was more expert at moving players from the crease than the six-foot-one Stanley, but he operated with surprising finesse. He never topped more than 70 penalty minutes, but his toughness was unquestioned. Stanley once played an entire game with a broken jaw after his face had been cut open by a skate.

Eventually, Stanley's influence extended to the entire blueline corps.

George Armstrong said, "Stanley and Horton were so successful that Carl Brewer and Bobby Baun said, 'We have to do what these guys are doing.' They mimicked him and it worked."

"Allan was the boss of that pair," said Armstrong. "He told Tim when to go and when not to go. Allan Stanley was the brains of our defence."

Phil Esposito with Allan Stanley in hot pursuit

TERRY SAWCHUK

GOALTENDER • 1964–65 TO 1966–67

Born: **December 28, 1929, Winnipeg, Manitoba** Died: **May 31, 1970 (40), New York, New York**
Games: **91** Wins: **42** Losses: **29** Ties: **14** Shutouts: **4** Goals against: **2.81**
Stanley Cup: **1967**
Awards: **Vezina Trophy, 1965**
Inducted into Hockey Hall of Fame: **1971**

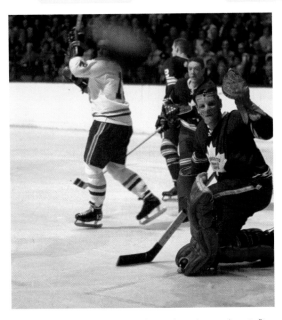

Terry Sawchuk watches the puck as it flies
toward the camera

It was Game 4 of the 1967 Stanley Cup semi-finals and Terry Sawchuk, nursing a throbbing shoulder, was called in to relieve the injured Johnny Bower. A few seconds after play resumed, Bobby Hull unleashed a slap shot that rocketed into Sawchuk's upper body. He went down like a felled tree.

"Are you all right?" asked the Leafs trainer upon reaching Sawchuk.

"I stopped the puck, didn't I?" he snarled.

Terry Sawchuk is one of the prominent architects of the Leafs' 1967 Cup triumph. He stopped 41 shots in the final game, a 3–1 win, but for Sawchuk, a sour and often angry man, it was like every shot peeled off a layer of skin.

"You had to understand him," said Marcel Pronovost, a teammate of Sawchuk's in Detroit and Toronto. "I roomed with Terry for years. When he got up in the morning, I would say hello. If he answered, we'd talk the rest of the day. If he didn't answer, I just kept quiet."

"I got along fine with him," said defenceman Bob Baun, "but yes, yes, he was an eccentric. To be a goalie playing at that time, without a mask, you had to be an eccentric."

Terry Sawchuk's assent to the NHL was in a way a tribute to the brother he lost at an early age. His brother Mike was the goaltender in the family, but when the older sibling he idolized died suddenly of a heart ailment, Terry donned the pads. Sawchuk's ambition was ferocious. He refused to go

Allan Stanley tries to slow up a Black Hawk for Terry Sawchuk

to movies as a young man because he was afraid eye strain would diminish his vision. Sawchuk won the Calder Trophy for rookie of the year with the Wings in 1951. He would win three Vezina Trophies as the league's best goalie and share a fourth one with Bower in 1965.

His style was frenetic. Newspaperman Dick Beddoes wrote: "To watch him make a save was to wonder who did the choreography, out went the arm, over went the stick, up with the glove to catch the puck and throw it into the corner, all in such swift succession that he was a long padded blur."

When Terry Sawchuk died in 1970, the Hall of Fame waived its three-year waiting period, and the magnificent goalie, a four-time Stanley Cup winner, was inducted a few months later.

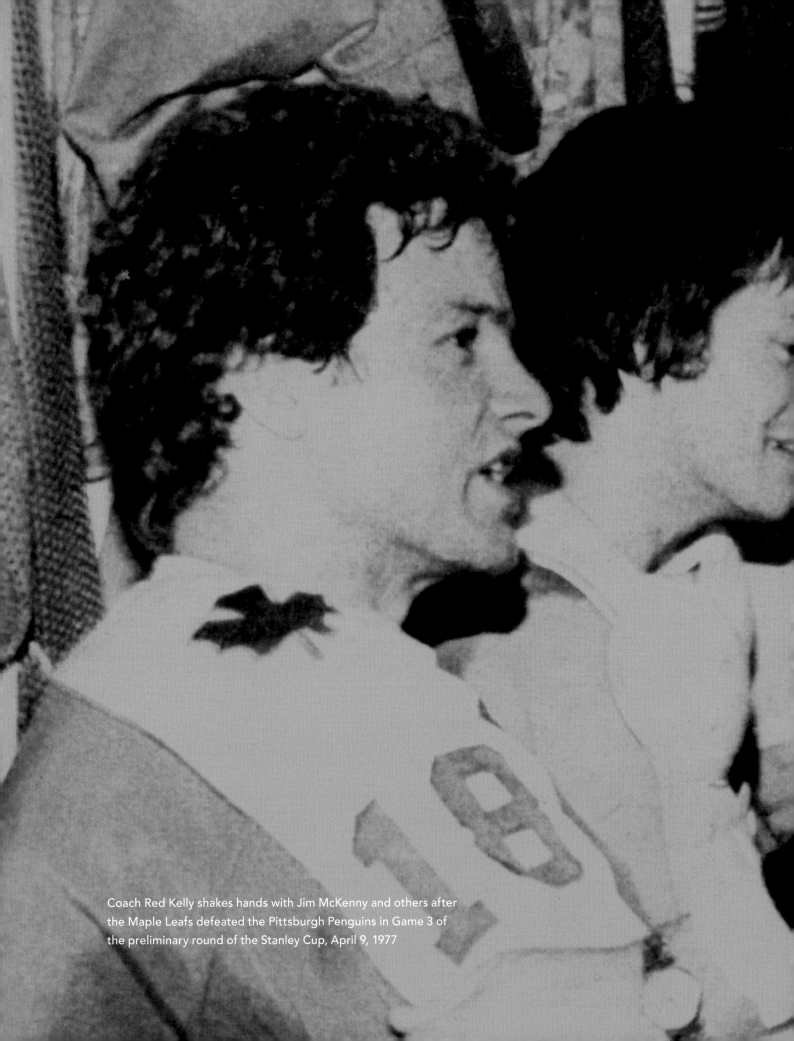

Coach Red Kelly shakes hands with Jim McKenny and others after the Maple Leafs defeated the Pittsburgh Penguins in Game 3 of the preliminary round of the Stanley Cup, April 9, 1977

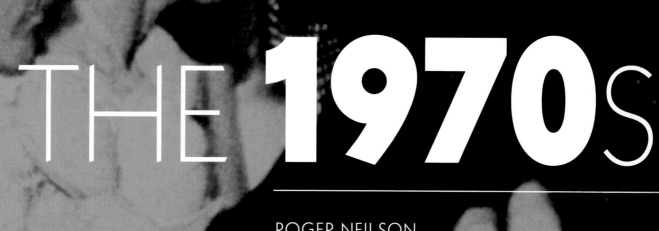

THE **1970**s

ROGER NEILSON

BRIAN GLENNIE

ERROL THOMPSON

IAN TURNBULL

JACQUES PLANTE

JIM McKENNY

INGE HAMMARSTROM

RON ELLIS

PAUL HENDERSON

NORM ULLMAN

DAVE "TIGER" WILLIAMS

MIKE PALMATEER

LANNY McDONALD

JIM GREGORY

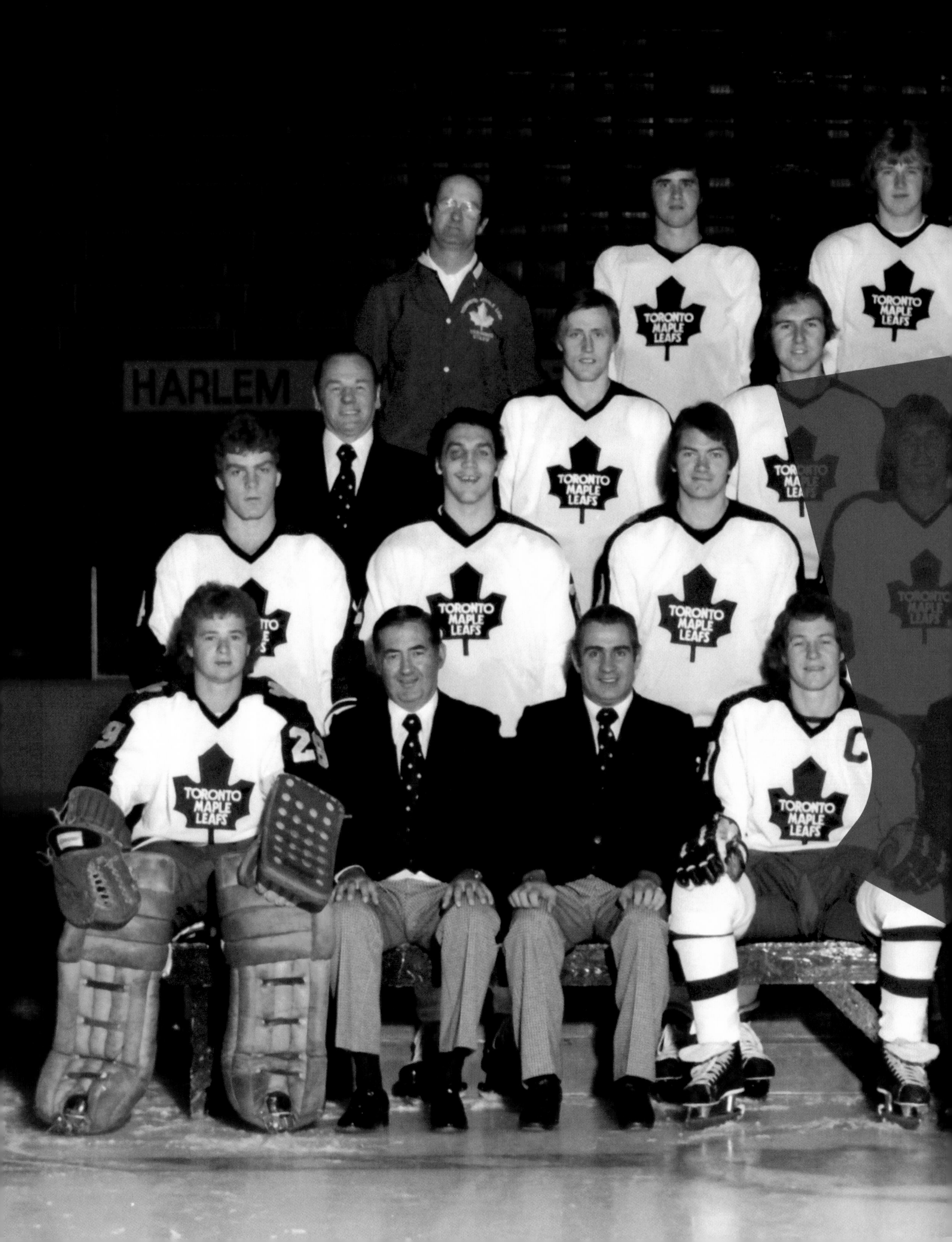
HARLEM
TORONTO
MAPLE
LEAFS
29
C

TEAM OF THE DECADE
1977–78 TORONTO MAPLE LEAFS

REGULAR SEASON RECORD: 41-29-10

PLAYOFF RECORD: 6-7

The 1977–78 Leafs staged one of the biggest upsets in franchise history, upending the New York Islanders, 18 points better in the regular season, in seven games.

The series featured two teams with comparable casts but radically different futures. The Islanders, who would claim the first of four straight Stanley Cups two years later, were led by centre Bryan Trottier, hard-hitting Clark Gillies, gifted scorer Mike Bossy, and sparkplug goalie Billy Smith.

The Leafs boasted a comparable group led by 27-year-old Darryl Sittler, who was coming off his best regular season with 45 goals and 117 points. Lanny McDonald, who scored the series-winning goal, hit for 47 goals, and the third member of the number-one unit, muckraker Tiger Williams, banked 19 goals and 50 points. The team had a core of veteran leadership that included 33-year-old Ron Ellis.

While he would be lost partway through the playoffs due to an eye injury, Borje Salming was coming off a 76-point season. In his absence, Ian Turnbull played the best hockey of his career, leading the Leafs in playoff scoring with six goals and 16 points in just 13 games. Rookie coach Roger Neilson assembled a hard-working supporting cast including Pat Boutette, Jimmy Jones, and Jerry Butler. Goalie Mike Palmateer was rarely better.

In spite of this potential, the Leafs would be swept by a powerhouse Montreal Canadiens team in the third round. A year later, Leafs owner Harold Ballard dismissed Neilson and general manager Jim Gregory. The most promising team of the decade would soon be disassembled.

ROGER NEILSON

 COACH • 1977–78/1978–79

Born: **June 16, 1934, Toronto, Ontario** Died: **June 21, 2003 (69), Peterborough, Ontario**
Games: **160** Record: **75 W, 62 L, 23 T** Pts. %: **.541** Pts. %: **.541**
Inducted into Hockey Hall of Fame: **2002 (Builder)**

Roger Neilson, 1977, Montreal Forum

Despite the glories of the Doug Gilmour Leafs of the early 1990s and the Mats Sundin–led club of a decade later, it is a point of fact for veteran Leafs fans that the team's greatest chance for a Stanley Cup after 1967 came with a curly-haired former high school teacher behind the bench.

"Roger Neilson was the finest coach I ever had," said Darryl Sittler. "He made everyone feel whatever their role was in the organization mattered. His teams were always ready. Accountability was one of his biggest things. He demanded it and guys loved playing for him."

Roger Neilson was, from the beginning, an eccentric, in part because of the unconventional nature of his ideas, in part because the hockey world could not yet grasp his brilliance. Neilson lived in track suits and a baseball cap but took pride in wearing the most garish necktie behind the bench. His dog, Mike, was his only real constant companion. Sometimes during practice, Neilson would position Mike in front of the net and instruct him to sit. Naturally, Mike didn't leave his position in front of the net to overextend the forecheck. If Mike the dog knew enough not to go behind the net, Roger preached, a grown man could do the same.

He began the practice of contacting players through the off-season to ensure they were staying in condition. He was one of the first to videotape games for scouting and coaching. He hired an assistant, Ron Wilson, thought to be the league's first true assistant coach.

He asked his goalies, Mike Palmateer and Gord McRae, to write reports on every goal scored against them and how they could improve.

And while his principles were absolute, he ceded an unprecedented amount of power to his players. A committee, comprised of Darryl Sittler, Ron Ellis, and Borje Salming, conferred with the players to set up everything from travel arrangements to practice schedules.

Neilson's 1977–78 team went 41-29-10. The team had never won that many games before and would not for 15 more seasons. But that would be as good as it got. When the Leafs failed to build on that success in 1979, Leafs owner Harold Ballard fired Neilson. But the players' demanded his return and Ballard acceded. The decision was made just minutes before a game on Saturday, March 1, and Neilson appeared behind the bench to cheers from spectators and fans alike.

However, Neilson's stay was not long. After that season, he left and went on to coach in Buffalo, Vancouver, Chicago, New York, Florida, and Philadelphia. Neilson died of cancer in 2003 at 69. By then, many of his maverick ways had evolved into common practice, and as his associations inside the game deepened, so too did the love many players felt for him. Without winning a single Stanley Cup, he was nonetheless as influential as any Cup-winning coach and had earned the love of many of his players.

"The thing about Roger," former Toronto Marlies coach Dallas Eakins once said, "is that I truly believed I was one of his best friends. And I was. But so was everybody else."

24

BRIAN GLENNIE

DEFENCE • 1969–70 TO 1977–78

Born: **August 29, 1946, Toronto, Ontario**
Games: **554** Goals: **12** Assists: **98** Points: **110** PIMs: **599**

Brian Glennie and Stan Mikita of the Chicago Black Hawks

The joke was that Leafs defenceman Brian Glennie had a medical file that took two people to lift. He had surgeries on both shoulders, broke his nose half-a-dozen times, had his jaw split open, and endured a herniated disk and assorted sundry breaks including his cheekbones and ankles.

Glennie was one of the final practitioners of the hip check. The hip check was difficult to execute but devastatingly effective. It involved the defending player hitting an oncoming opponent at the hip and lifting the player off the ice with his rump. If the point of contact was too low, the hip check could savage a player's knees. Invariably it took a toll on Glennie, who would sometimes hand out as many as 20 hits, many of them hip checks, a game.

"You have to time it just right," Glennie once explained. "If you go out looking for hits, you can get yourself out of position very easily. But I get a lot of satisfaction out of hitting. You know when you've got a good one and so does the guy who's getting it."

Glennie was a true defensive defenceman. He scored

Brian Glennie, March 12, 1974, St. Louis Arena

only 14 goals in 574 games as a Leaf, but had there been a category for blocked shots, Glennie would have been among the league leaders every year. His courage was so well known that Team Canada selected him for the 1972 Summit Series.

Despite his habit of inflicting damage on opposing players, Glennie earned league-wide respect for his competitiveness. He was a clean player who averaged about one minor penalty every two games.

Canadiens forward Rejean Houle was asked why he didn't retaliate after one of Glennie's signature hip checks sent him flying. "How could I get mad?" Houle said. "It was a clean check. Glennie is one of the few guys who can do it without throwing in a little stick or elbow. It was clean but it still hurt."

ERROL
THOMPSON

LEFT WING • 1970–71/1972–73 TO 1977–78

Born: **May 28, 1950, Summerside, Prince Edward Island**
Games: **365** Goals: **126** Assists: **119** Points: **597** PIMs: **70**

Errol Thompson had planned to quit. He loved hockey, but when you are born in Summerside, Prince Edward Island, the pipelines to the NHL are far less accessible than they are for a boy from Ontario or Quebec.

"I just got to the point in time as an 18-year-old where I was undecided in what I wanted to do," he once said. "Finally, I decided I didn't want to play hockey anymore."

Instead, Thompson was talked into playing defence for $30 a game for a senior team in Charlottetown. He hauled furniture for a moving company to pay his bills.

In the days before scouting combines and tiers of talent evaluators, a player's career was sometimes furthered or even born by word of mouth or sheer luck. Leafs scout Johnny Bower got word of Thompson and instantly became entranced, as so many would, by his superb skating. The Leafs drafted Thompson 22nd overall in 1970.

He was so star-struck that on his first trip to the Gardens that a staffer mistook Thompson for a fan and turfed him from the arena. By his third Leafs campaign, Thompson was a 25-goal scorer. He scored 43 goals one season playing on a line with Darryl Sittler and Lanny McDonald. That season, the kid from Prince Edward Island was the 10th highest goalscorer in the NHL.

Errol Thompson takes a shot on Ken Dryden of the Montreal Canadiens

A straight-line skater and a straight-shooter, Thompson was matter-of-fact about his game. "I have no finesse. I couldn't go one on one against my wife and come out ahead," he said. "But I can go fast all night."

Thompson broke his arm after his big year but still scored 21 goals in half a season. Eventually the Leafs felt they needed to trade speed for toughness, and Thompson was dealt to Detroit for hard-rock forward Dan Maloney.

Thompson just kept on scoring. He ended up recording at least 20 goals in nine straight NHL seasons but retired at 31 with some bounce still left in his legs.

"I said when I started that I was going to leave when I wanted to leave not when they wanted me to," Errol Thompson said. "I had 11 years of professional hockey and that's something I can be very happy with."

IAN
TURNBULL

DEFENCE • 1973–74 TO 1981–82

Born: **December 22, 1953, Pointe-Claire, Quebec**
Games: **580** Goals: **112** Assists: **302** Points: **414** PIMs: **651**

The pass, said Darryl Sittler, was almost always the same: hard and on the tape. "Ian Turnbull was a great passer," Sittler said. "He could see the ice, and when he and Borje [Salming] were together, they were one of the best twosomes in the league."

The mastery of a tape-to-tape pass to a streaking winger was just one of Turnbull's gifts. Turnbull departed Toronto in 1982 as the all-time goals leader among Leafs rearguards. It took Tim Horton 21 years to set the previous standard of 110 goals. Turnbull broke the mark in eight seasons, but the tumult of those years, punctuated by the eccentricities and dictates of owner Harold Ballard, wore him down.

Turnbull set a record that still stands: five goals in a 9–1 win over the Detroit Red Wings at Maple Leaf Gardens, February 2, 1977.

Turnbull was 23 when he set the standard and he scored in every way that seemed possible. One goal banked off Detroit defenceman Terry Harper past Wings netminder Ed Giacomin. Two of the goals were results of breakaways. On another he carried the puck into the net as he was sent sprawling through the crease. Another came on a point shot.

"A couple of the goals were easy," said Turnbull candidly. "A couple were lucky."

"He was the whole game," said Detroit coach Larry Wilson. "He did us in by himself."

Turnbull entered the game in the grip of a terrible scoring slump that was approaching 30 games. It was a mystifying drought for a player whose offensive skills and willingness to attack were among the league's most pronounced.

At times jarringly candid, Turnbull all but traded himself. His play bottomed out near the end of his eight-and-a-half-year stint. "Everybody in Toronto knew years ago that I should have been gone. I knew it. I just lost that edge, didn't have the motivation," he said after being traded to Los Angeles for journeyman Billy Harris.

Ian Turnbull skates against Bobby Schmautz of the Boston Bruins at the Boston Garden

The pastures would never be as green for Turnbull again. He played just 48 more NHL games, and he was out of the league before his 30th birthday. He finished plus 55 in 1976–77 and was never more dazzling than he was that spring when he filled the void created by an injury to Borje Salming and helped lead the Leafs to a seven-game upset of the New York Islanders.

Turnbull would later say the five-goal night changed his career for the worse by creating a standard he could never reach, but he is remembered by fans as one of the most offensively gifted rearguards to play for the Leafs.

JACQUES
PLANTE

 GOALTENDER • 1970–71 TO 1972–73

Born: **January 17, 1929, Notre-Dame-du-Mont-Carmel, Quebec**
Died: **February 27, 1986 (57), Geneva, Switzerland**
Games: **106** Wins: **48** Losses: **38** Ties: **15** Shutouts: **7** Goals against: **2.46**
Inducted into Hockey Hall of Fame: **1978**

Jacques Plante played for the Leafs for three years in the early 1970s and was formidable even in his early 40s. In his third season with the Leafs, he went 15-15-6 with a 2.81 goals against average. He was 44 years old.

Goalies are often considered a superstitious, individualistic and unique group. Even by these standards, Jacques Plante was an eccentric. He roomed alone and always sat apart in the first row of the bus where he knitted toques and socks.

Perhaps this is part of what made him an innovator. Plante is the father of the goalie mask. And any goalie who corrals a loose puck in his end and passes it to a streaking forward is paying homage to Plante, the first of the wandering goalies.

He was relentless in his pursuit of perfection. He studied the game and honed his own skills in response. His scientific approach to his position was formalized in his book, *On Goaltending*.

Plante was often racked with asthma, which he said flared up in planes, hotel rooms, and even in particular

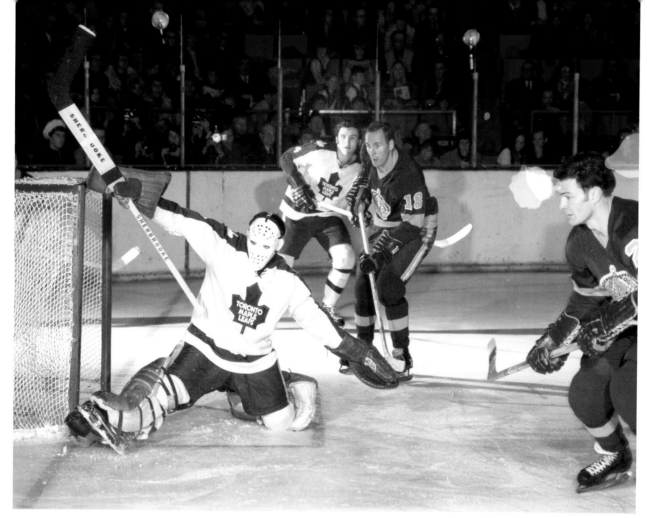

Jacques Plante kicks out the shot

cities. One of those cities was Toronto, but the Leafs placated Plante with an apartment on the outskirts, away from the heavier air that Plante claimed cloaked the interior of the city.

While he was generous in his advice with young goalies, Plante did not often consort with position players. He never trusted a hockey player who didn't wear goalie pads.

Plante's independent ways often put him in conflict with his coaches. He wore his face mask, his greatest innovation, in defiance of his coach, the Canadiens' fiery Toe Blake.

"I never make friends, not in hockey, not elsewhere, not since I was a teenager," he once said. "What for? If you are close to someone you must be scheduling yourself to please them. Maybe it was the asthma, the fact I need more rest than anybody else, but I have always kept my own schedule."

"Nobody knew him in Toronto," the garrulous defenceman Jim McKenny once said. "We never saw him except at games and practices."

Plante finally retired at 46. While his 3.32 goals against average that year was a career high, Plante's pride still shone brightly.

Best to go, he told reporters, before age began to diminish his skills. And it was those extraordinary skills that carved out a storied career by one of hockey's greatest innovators.

Jim McKenny (right) and Yvan Cournoyer

JIM MCKENNY

DEFENCE • 1965–66 TO 1977–78

Born: **December 1, 1946, Ottawa, Ontario**
Games: **594** Goals: **81** Assists: **246** Points: **327** PIMs: **292**

Everyone loved Jim McKenny.

"Truly one of the funniest men ever to play," said Lanny McDonald.

McKenny was nicknamed "Howie," a reference to Howie Young, himself one of the league's wildest characters and a player who, like McKenny, turned beet red with exertion during games.

McKenny raised self-deprecation to an art form. An offensive defenceman with a penchant for risky moves, McKenny had been compared in junior with Bobby Orr. "I was supposed to be the next Bobby Orr and it ruined me," McKenny deadpanned. "I guess I was a rebel, but I really never knew what I was rebelling against."

Veering in front of his own net was a common McKenny move. "It used to drive goalies crazy," he said. "I can still hear Jacques Plante swearing at me in French from behind his mask. [Leafs goalie] Doug Favell once told me that when I played in front of him, he didn't get out of his crouch for three years."

On being benched: "Those back-to-back games will kill you. They're very hard on the throat."

To a visitor at Leafs practice: "I can't talk to you now but come down during the game."

It was McKenny's defensive shortcomings that brought about the end of his Leafs career. Leafs coach Roger Neilson, a stickler for defence, couldn't live with McKenny's freewheeling ways.

"He used to make big red circles on his statistics sheet for every defensive giveaway and I had a thousand of them by Christmas," McKenny said. "Pretty soon I was up in the press box keeping stats myself."

Neilson was recasting the Leafs into a defensively sound team, and the high-risk, high-reward McKenny had no place in the new order. Leafs fans, though, loved McKenny's wildcat ways.

When he finally sent McKenny to the minors, GM Jim Gregory braced for the backlash. "He's a popular guy. I'll probably get a lot of flack," Gregory said. "Starting with my family."

INGE
HAMMARSTROM

LEFT WING • 1973–74 TO 1977–78

Born: **January 20, 1948, Sundsvall, Sweden**
Games: **292** Goals: **85** Assists: **82** Points: **167** PIMs: **74**

Inge Hammarstrom plays against the Boston Bruins
ca. 1970s

A brilliant skater and stickhandler, Inge Hammarstrom came to North America with a style that was out of step with the rough-house tactics that governed the 1970s-era NHL. While there were plenty of skilled, gentlemanly players to succeed in the NHL – such as Jean Ratelle and Yvan Cournoyer – Hammarstrom was perceived by some to be unwilling to fight for every inch of ice.

The NHL presented a different standard for European players, and Hammarstrom was one of the first. He arrived in Toronto with Borje Salming in 1972. The two were targets for players who would use brutish tactics in an attempt to scare the two Swedes into returning to their country and thus end what would be a migration of European hockey talent taking jobs Canadians felt were rightfully theirs.

"I felt sorry for him," said his teammate Darryl Sittler. "He was such a skilled player and players on the other teams would just abuse him. He would look at them as if they were crazy whereas Borje would fight back," Sittler said.

Hammarstrom scored 85 goals in five full seasons with the Leafs, but he was not a traditional tough guy.

"Even if I took lessons five times a week I could never be a fighter," he once said. "It was not in my nature."

Inge Hammarstrom, March 15, 1977, at St. Louis Arena

"It's too bad that he struggled so much with the physical play," longtime teammate Jim McKenny once said. "He had as much talent as anyone in our room."

Hammarstrom thrived when the Leafs matched talent with the NHL's best. "When we played Montreal I had my best games," he said. "It was satisfying to play them because they played the game the way it was supposed to be played. I loved to compete against guys like Yvan Cournoyer and Guy Lafleur."

The NHL is a radically different place today than when Hammarstrom arrived. Today's game values speed, élan, and skill more than ever. Unburdened by the pressure of being a pioneer, Inge Hammarstrom would have instead been allowed to shine as the star he was.

Ron Ellis received the #6 sweater to wear from Ace Bailey at the Hot Stove, Maple Leaf Gardens

RON ELLIS

RIGHT WING • 1963–64 TO 1974–75/1977–78 TO 1980–81

Born: **January 8, 1945, Lindsay, Ontario**
Games: **1,034** Goals: **332** Assists: **308** Points: **640** PIMs: **207**
Stanley Cup: **1967**

Even though he spent years under the unrelenting demands of Punch Imlach, Ron Ellis's toughest taskmaster would always be himself.

"When I was a young player, Ron Ellis was the player I watched," said Hall of Famer Lanny McDonald. "He was never satisfied with himself. Ron Ellis never stopped moving his legs and he never stopped giving. I wanted to be just like him."

Ellis played 11 seasons with the Leafs, retired in 1981, and then was wooed back for four more years.

Ellis was a powerful skater. His game was so uncannily steady that Toronto media took to calling him "Ron the Robot." In one stretch, he hit 20 goals in 9 of 10 seasons but in only of those seasons did he accrue a significant number of power-play goals. Everything Ron Ellis got he earned against the opposition's top players. Despite his defensive responsibilities, Ellis was on the plus side of the ledger in 13 of his 16 seasons.

"He was as good a defensive player as anyone could imagine," said his longtime linemate Paul Henderson.

The puck from Ron Ellis's first NHL goal

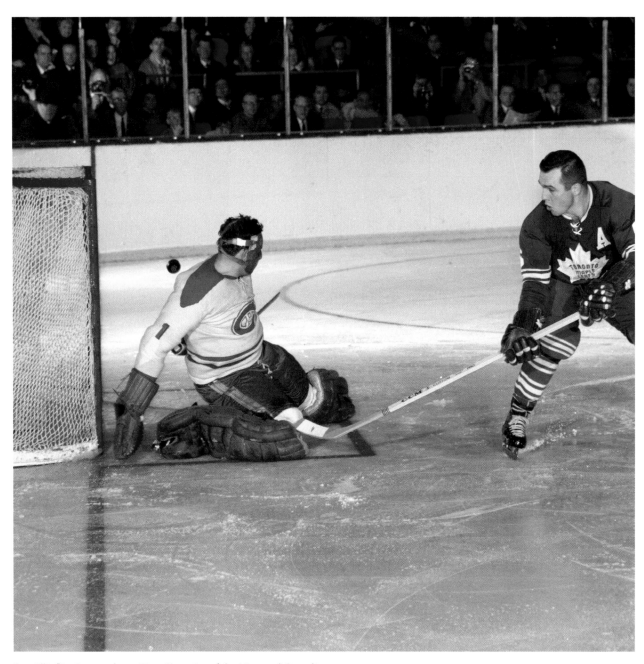

Ron Ellis flips in a goal past Tony Esposito of the Montreal Canadiens

"Any chance I took offensively I did knowing Ron was backing me up."

Ellis's game was so respected that he was chosen as a member of the 1972 Summit Series.

"I wanted to be known as a player who could score goals but could also be counted to check a big line or play the last few minutes of a close game," he said. "People said my style was robotic, but the people who paid my salary, my teammates and my opponents appreciated my style. That's all I could ever ask for."

PAUL HENDERSON

LEFT WINGER • 1967–68 TO 1973–74

Born: **January 28, 1943, Kincardine, Ontario**
Games: **408** Goals: **162** Assists: **156** Points: **318** PIMs: **166**

The biggest goal ever scored by a Maple Leaf wasn't scored for the Maple Leafs at all. When Paul Henderson scored his third consecutive game-winning goal in September 1972, he gave Team Canada a victory over a brilliant Soviet Union team and restored Canada's pride, first as a country and also as a hockey nation.

Dubbed the Summit Series, the eight-game meeting between Team Canada and the Soviets was supposed to be a rout. The Soviets had trampled the competition at the Olympics with their brilliant skating and passing; however, Canadians felt a hand-picked team of their professionals would dismantle their opponents. But the Soviets left the Canadian leg of the eight-game series with two wins, a loss, and a tie (Canada's only win came at the Gardens).

The Canadians needed a hero and they found one in Henderson, an industrious two-way winger who was coming off his best season, a 38-goal campaign. Henderson scored the game-winning goal in Games 6 and 7, and when Game 8 came down to its final moments, Canada's hopes for a victory seemed narrowly lost. That is, until Henderson shouted at a teammate from the bench.

"I called Peter Mahovlich off the ice moments before I scored the goal in Game 8," Henderson said. "I somehow had the feeling I would score that goal if I got the chance."

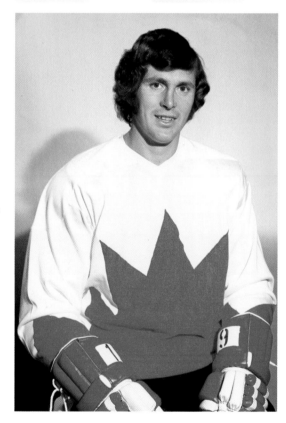

Paul Henderson in his official portrait as a member of Team Canada 1972

The Leafs play against the Boston Bruins during the 1968–69 season. From left: Don Awrey, Paul Henderson, and Phil Esposito

Henderson corralled a rebound and slipped the puck past Soviet goalie Vladislav Tretiak with just 34 seconds left and a nation rejoiced. When Team Canada touched down in Montreal, Prime Minister Pierre Trudeau was waiting to give congratulations from the country. The Canadians returned to a 50,000-person celebration in Toronto's Nathan Phillips Square.

"That goal was the highlight of my career," he would say later. "I had scored the goal my country needed when they needed it most."

Canadians never forgot the goal.

NORM ULLMAN

CENTRE • 1967–68 TO 1974–75

Born: **December 26, 1935, Provost, Alberta**
Games: **535** Goals: **166** Assists: **305** Points: **471** PIMs: **160**
Inducted into Hockey Hall of Fame: **1982**

They called Norm Ullman the mechanical man because of the precision of his game. A frequent linemate of Paul Henderson and Ron Ellis, Ullman was the prototypical centreman, conscientiously defensive, a smooth skater, and gifted playmaker.

A native of Provost, Ullman owned a fierce determination even as a child. When it was too cold for the other kids to venture out, Ullman would drag his hockey bag to the nearest rink and play until his feet were numb.

"His feet were so cold, he'd cry when his mother took his shoes off," his dad, John, once said. "She'd sit him in front of the oven to warm him up, but the next day he'd be out there again. Norm was a child who would rather play hockey than eat."

That dedication manifested itself in his complete game.

"With Norm, everything flowed from his defensive game," appraised Pat Quinn, a one-time teammate with the Leafs.

Ullman arrived in Toronto after 13 years with Detroit in the deal that sent Frank Mahovlich to the Red Wings.

"The way it worked out, it was great," said Ullman. "Punch Imlach thought a lot of me and insisted that I be in on the trade with Mahovlich. About a year later, he announced that I was the best centre he ever coached so that was quite a feather in my cap."

Norm Ullman in St. Louis, December 14, 1971

Norm Ullman and Gregg Sheppard of the Boston Bruins

He would put in seven years in Toronto playing a game born on the outdoor rink.

"When you watch Norm, he reminds you of a kid playing shinny," said Leafs teammate Bobby Baun. "It's like he's saying: this is my puck, get one of your own."

"Norm was the epitome of the great player, a great goalscorer, an incredible playmaker, and an amazing fore-checker," said Paul Henderson. "But at the end it was all about how much of a competitor he was. He brought it every single night."

22

DAVE "TIGER" WILLIAMS

LEFT WING • 1974–75 TO 1979–80

Born: **February 3, 1954, Weyburn, Saskatchewan**
Games: **407** Goals: **109** Assists: **132** Points: **241** PIMs: **1,670**

The natural order of things changed the moment 20-year-old Dave "Tiger" Williams arrived at Maple Leafs camp in 1974. He was asked about the players he would be competing against for a spot on the roster. "I think the other guys should worry about me instead of me worrying about them," he told reporters. "I'm here to make it."

And he did.

There was nothing new in this. His ferocious personality earned him the nickname "Tiger" when Dave Williams was only eight years old. Nor did the plan for his life ever waver. When he was a grade-10 student back home in Weyburn, Saskatchewan, a guidance instructor asked him to jot down his career aspirations. Dave Williams wrote three letters: "NHL."

Tiger was schooled in fighting by his older brother Morgan, a national level boxer. "With five brothers I learned how to look after myself," Williams once said. "My brothers hit me so hard I still might have lumps on my head."

He worked on oil rigs in Alberta when he was 15 years old. "It was brutal work, 16-hour days," he said. "One time I worked a stretch of 44 straight days without a day off. That business either toughened you up or killed you."

Williams spent six years on the left side of a line with Darryl Sittler and Lanny McDonald and had two seasons of 20-plus goals and one 30-goal year. The thought of being an offensive player tickled Williams. "It's pretty heady stuff for a guy like me. Usually I'm checking someone, now they're checking me," he said. "When I do something right it shows up on the scoreboard because of what Darryl and Lanny can do."

Tiger Williams, one of the Leafs' great roughnecks, would tell you there are much tougher places to hold your own than a hockey rink. "Who gets hurt in a hockey fight?" Tiger once said. "The worst you get is a couple of stitches and a bloody nose."

MIKE
PALMATEER

Born: **January 13, 1954, Toronto, Ontario**
Games: **296** Wins: **129** Losses: **112** Ties: **41** Shutouts: **15** Goals against: **3.43**

Mike Palmateer, when he played for the Oklahoma City
Blazers of the Central Hockey League (ca. 1975)

Before goaltending became a game of being hit by the puck instead of going to find it, there was a breed of undersized, spectacular goalies: Rogie Vachon in Los Angeles, Eddie Giacomin in New York, and in Toronto, the dazzling Mike Palmateer.

Palmateer stood only five foot nine and weighed just 170 pounds. On tiptoes, he barely crested above the knob of tape at the end of Ken Dryden's goal stick. But his brazen play made him seem bigger.

"He was a colourful guy," said Darryl Sittler, a teammate and co-author of the Leafs' hallowed 1978 upset of the New York Islanders. "He played with a lot of confidence and that rubbed off on the other guys, on the teams playing him, and the fans watching him."

When Palmateer arrived in Toronto in 1976 with 81 minor league games in his pocket, he told general manager Jim Gregory to put any worries aside, Gregory's search for a stopper was over.

"I may be totally wrong but I think I'm one of the best," Palmateer once told a journalist. "A goaltender can have a lot of talent but if he doesn't think he can do the job every night, doesn't think he can make the big save, then he's had it."

Palmateer recklessly confronted shooters and then taunted them after he made a stop. "It's great to rob a guy," Palmateer said, "and tell him he's a lousy shooter."

Mike Palmateer defends against Clark Gillies of the New York Islanders

There were no routine saves in Palmateer's arsenal. "Somehow he would make an easy save look difficult just because of how acrobatic he was," Sittler said.

"Me, I destroy my body every time I play. I'm up and down, I'm rolling around and I'm getting hit because I'm challenging," Palmateer once said. "That's the way I play, I attack. But it's hard to say how long I can play. I hope I can last 15 years."

Instead he was done at 31 after just eight NHL seasons. Palmateer's style was built for excitement, not longevity, but he delivered a lifetime's worth of memorable saves as a Leaf.

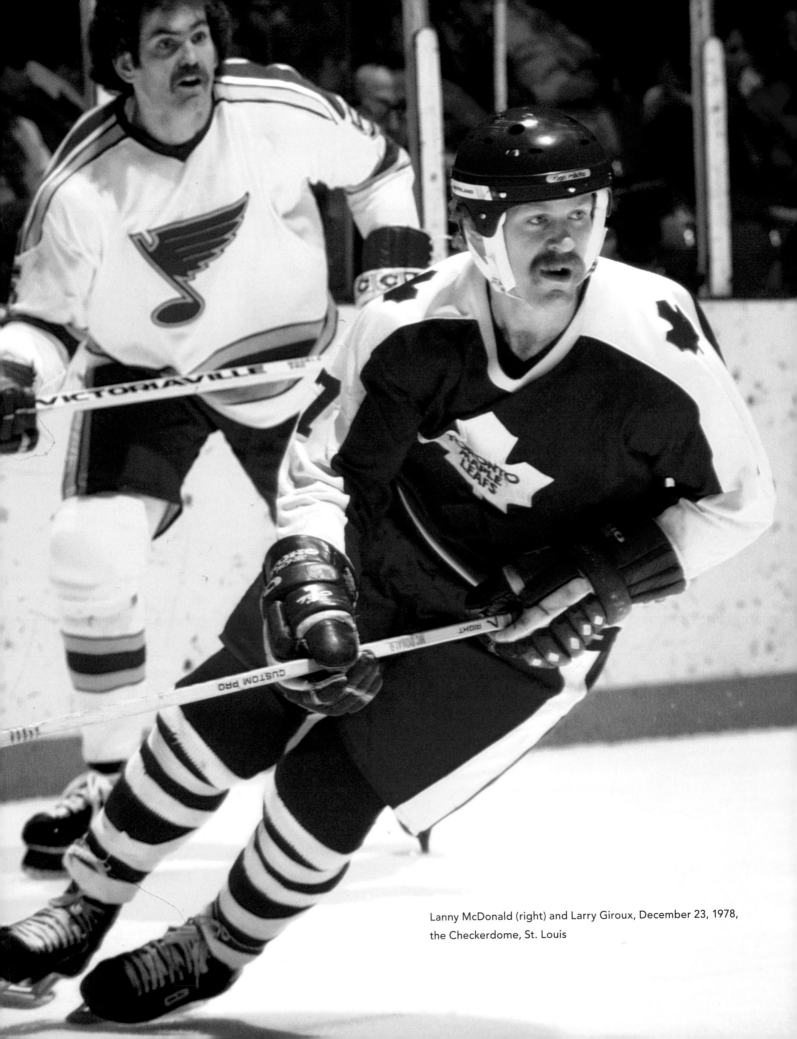

Lanny McDonald (right) and Larry Giroux, December 23, 1978,
the Checkerdome, St. Louis

LANNY McDONALD

RIGHT WING • 1973–74 TO 1979–80

Born: **February 16, Hanna, Alberta**
Games: **477** Goals: **219** Assists: **240** Points: **459** PIMs: **372**
Inducted into Hockey Hall of Fame: **1992**

Lanny authored a five-season run where he never scored fewer than 37 goals. He accomplished nearly all of that on a line with Darryl Sittler, a reliable playmaker expert at getting the puck in spots where McDonald could unleash his jaw-dropping wrist shot. There is no count on how many times Sittler won a faceoff and drew the puck back to McDonald for a rapid-fire goal.

"Lanny was an all-around complete player," Sittler said. "He could play it tough, hit in the corners, bodycheck, but he had that famous shot when he came down the wing."

No goal was bigger than the one McDonald scored to eliminate the New York Islanders in overtime in 1977, but when Imlach returned to his second tour of duty in Toronto, he decided to rid the team of Sittler.

Sittler's no-trade clause made that impossible, so Imlach did the next best thing and traded McDonald to Colorado. Leafs fans picketed the building when the deal was announced, and a crestfallen Sittler would soon cut the C from his jersey and quit his captaincy.

McDonald thrived, though, and pieced together a Hall of Fame career that included a 66-goal season in Calgary, where he won a Stanley Cup in 1989.

JIM
GREGORY

 GENERAL MANAGER • 1969–79

Born: **November 4, 1935, Dunnville, Ontario**
Games: **788** Record: **334 W, 324 L, 130 T** Pts. %: **.506**
Inducted into Hockey Hall of Fame: **2007 (Builder)**

For Jim Gregory, a Leafs fan from the small town of Dunnville, Ontario, the Maple Leafs were a gateway to a rich life in hockey. Gregory was an astute administrator, coach, and recruiter who guided two Toronto Marlboro teams to Memorial Cup victories as the top junior clubs in Canada.

In 1968, the Leafs hired Gregory as a scout, and a year later they tapped him to be their general manager. The Leafs would qualify for the playoffs in eight of Gregory's 10 seasons. Gregory was one of the first league executives to recognize Europe as a formidable source of NHL talent. Under his watch, the Leafs landed Hall of Fame defenceman Borje Salming, among the very first Europeans to thrive in the NHL.

Fired by owner Harold Ballard after the Leafs were eliminated by a powerhouse Islanders squad in 1979, Gregory was out of work for two days before being hired by the NHL as director of scouting. Gregory distinguished himself as the executive director of hockey operations for the league and later became a longtime chair of the Hockey Hall of Fame's selection committee. When he withdrew from the committee for a year because of illness in 2007, the remaining members voted him into the Hall of Fame as a builder.

Honoured Members Borje Salming and Jim Gregory, November 12, 2011

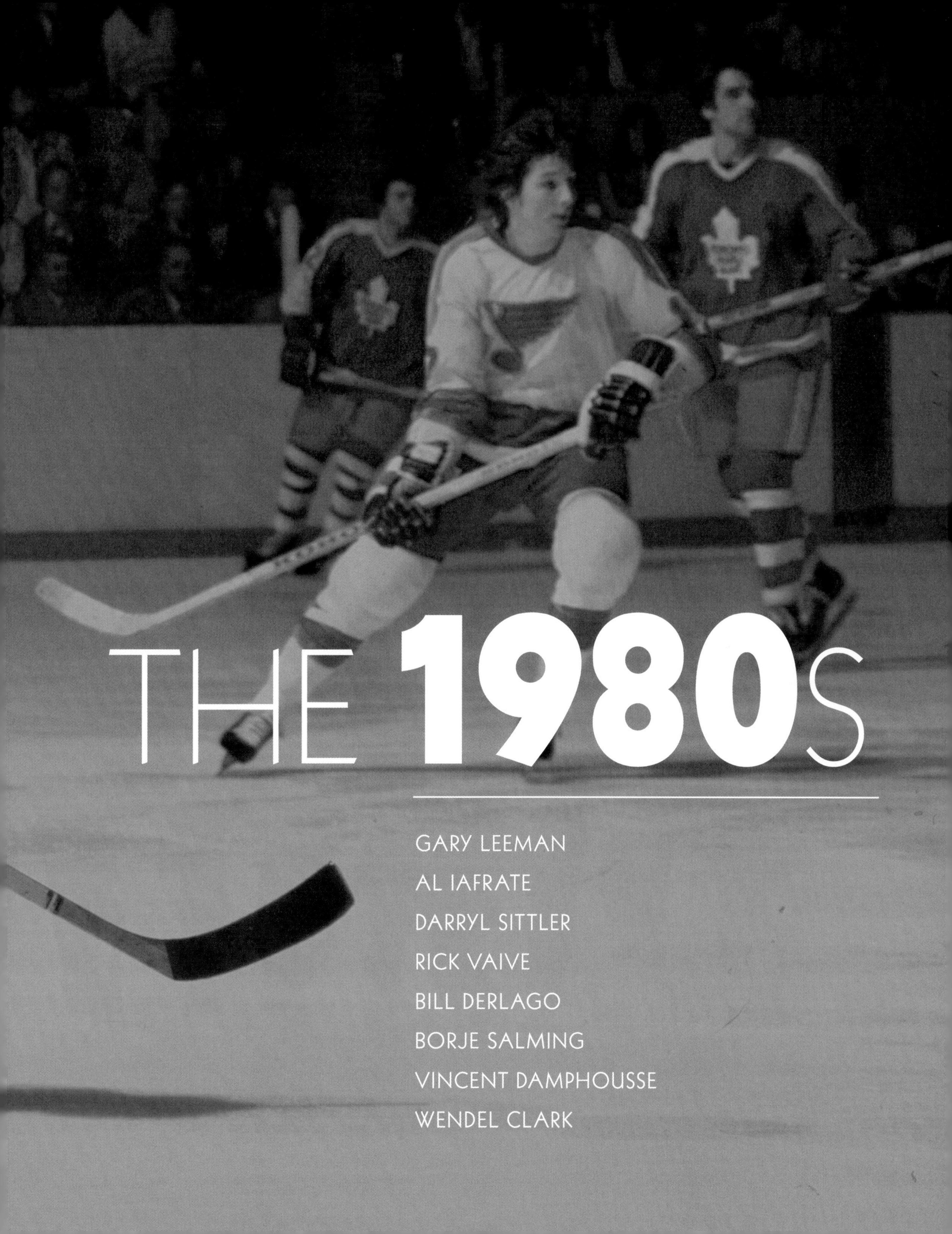

THE 1980s

GARY LEEMAN

AL IAFRATE

DARRYL SITTLER

RICK VAIVE

BILL DERLAGO

BORJE SALMING

VINCENT DAMPHOUSSE

WENDEL CLARK

TEAM OF THE DECADE
1986–87 TORONTO MAPLE LEAFS

———————

REGULAR SEASON RECORD: 32-42-6
PLAYOFF RECORD: 7-6

Coached by the incendiary John Brophy, the 1986–87 Leafs were a team with a cast of young, talented forwards. No Leafs team would feature more players hitting the 20-goal mark than the seven Leafs who hit the standard: Wendel Clark (a team-leading 37 goals), Steve Thomas (35), Rick Vaive (32), Russ Courtnall (29), Gary Leeman, Tom Fergus, and Vincent Damphousse (all three with 21).

The Leafs beat the St. Louis Blues in six games to advance into the second round. Toronto then lost a 3–1 lead in games to fall to Detroit in seven.

GARY LEEMAN

RIGHT WING • 1983–84 TO 1991–92

Born: **February 19, 1964, Wilcox, Saskatchewan**
Games: **545** Goals: **176** Assists: **231** Points: **407** PIMs: **463**

Gary Leeman was the second Leaf to score 50 goals, and a key player in the deal that brought Doug Gilmour to the Maple Leafs in 1992.

From an early age, Leeman exhibited a natural athletic ability and a broad skillset. He was usually the best athlete on any team in which he played, he was a scratch golfer, and a talented artist, and he also taught himself to play piano by ear. Drafted as a defenceman, Leeman played every position but goal in Toronto.

He was often teamed with fellow Notre Dame College alumni Wendel Clark and Russ Courtnall on the Hound Line – a reference to the nickname of the tiny Saskatchewan school all three players attended.

Leeman twice hit the 30-goal marker as a Leaf and recorded four seasons of 20-plus goals but his career peaked when he scored his 50th in March of 1991 with a goal against the New York Islanders matching Rick Vaive's record. Leeman became the first forward drafted as a defenceman to hit the 50-goal standard and his feat of 135 goals struck over four seasons was among the most productive periods for any Leaf goalscorer.

Though he won a Stanley Cup in 1992 playing with Montreal, Leeman never enjoyed the same level of offensive success after he left Toronto as a series of injuries curtailed his effectiveness.

"I was lucky enough to play in the two flagships cities of the NHL," Leeman said of Toronto and Montreal.

AL IAFRATE

33

DEFENCE • 1984–85 TO 1990–91

Born: **March 21, 1966, Dearborn, Michigan**
Games: **472** Goals: **81** Assists: **169** Points: **250** PIMs: **546**

Al Iafrate was a wild child, a Harley-Davidson–riding, tattooed defenceman with spectacular skating and shooting skills. "There were a lot of nicknames," Iafrate once said. "Wild Thing, the Human Highlight Reel, Planet Iafrate. They were all fun."

Drafted fourth overall in 1984, Iafrate stood six foot three and carried 235 pounds, and when he torqued that mass into a shot he inspired awe. He won the 1994 All-Star Game with a slapshot of 105.2 mph. No one else was even close.

"Al was a different guy, but Al was also a terrific person," said longtime Leafs teammate Bob McGill. "He was the sort of teammate who couldn't do enough for the guy beside him."

There was no limit to his talent or his individuality. In his fourth season, Iafrate scored 22 goals and had 52 points in 77 games. His total would have been higher, but Iafrate refused to shoot at the opposing net when the goalie was pulled. "Empty-net goals are for losers," he said.

One year, upset over Iafrate's rapid weight gain, the Leafs subjected Iafrate to an extra long training camp. He was typically unapologetic. "I spent too much time this summer with the girl next door," he said. "She happens to be my grandmother, one of the world's greatest Italian cooks."

DARRYL SITTLER

CENTRE • 1970–71 TO 1981–82 **C**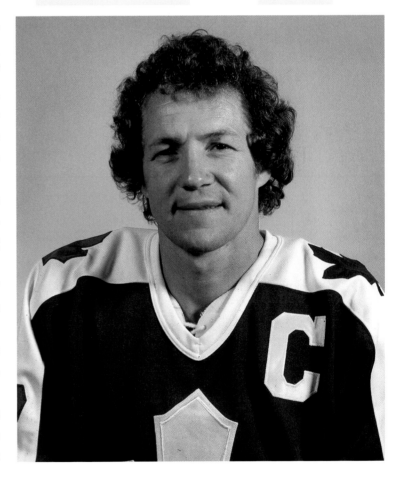

Born: **September 18, 1950, Kitchener, Ontario**
Games: **844** Goals: **389** Assists: **527** Points: **916** PIMs **763**
Inducted into Hockey Hall of Fame: **1989**

D arryl Sittler gained his Hall of Fame career through an unending thirst for work and competition. His drive was no doubt born of his early life. Sittler grew up one of eight children in St. Jacobs, Ontario. Darryl had two shirts and two pairs of pants for the school week. He paid for his hockey equipment scooping horse droppings off the main street.

"I worked with the Mennonite people. You were paid three bucks a day and you ate three solid meals," he once said. "Picking potatoes and in the fall picking apples, cleaning out pig manure in the barns."

Drafted eighth overall in 1970, Sittler quickly carved out a position of leadership on the Leafs. He was named captain at 24 and wore the letter for six seasons.

"Darryl was always the hardest-working guy on the team," appraised his onetime coach Roger Neilson. "When the captain does that, it picks everybody up."

Never a first all-star, Sittler played in an era of great centremen: Phil Esposito, Wayne Gretzky, and Bryan Trottier. Sittler was a well-rounded player. He was a

Darryl Sittler (left) and Ian Turbull, December 23, 1978. Toronto beat St. Louis 6–1

Hall of Famer because of the breadth of his talents and the fierceness of his competitive drive.

"What you see with Darryl is what you get," his longtime linemate Lanny McDonald wrote in his memoir. "If you go down fighting, whether it be a seventh game or with friendships, when the final buzzer goes you know he'll still be there."

In the late 1970s, the Leafs – powered by Sittler, McDonald, Ian Turnbull, Borje Salming, and Mike Palmateer – were one of the league's bright young teams. Ballard's decision to return Punch Imlach set up a struggle for control of the Leafs dressing room. The conflict resulted in Sittler resigning his captaincy, but by then his place as one of the Leafs' great leaders was already cemented.

Sittler might not have managed a Stanley Cup final but his achievements earned him a devoted following. Most notably he scored the winning goal in the 1976 Canada Cup tournament and his 10 points in a 1976 game against Boston remains a league record.

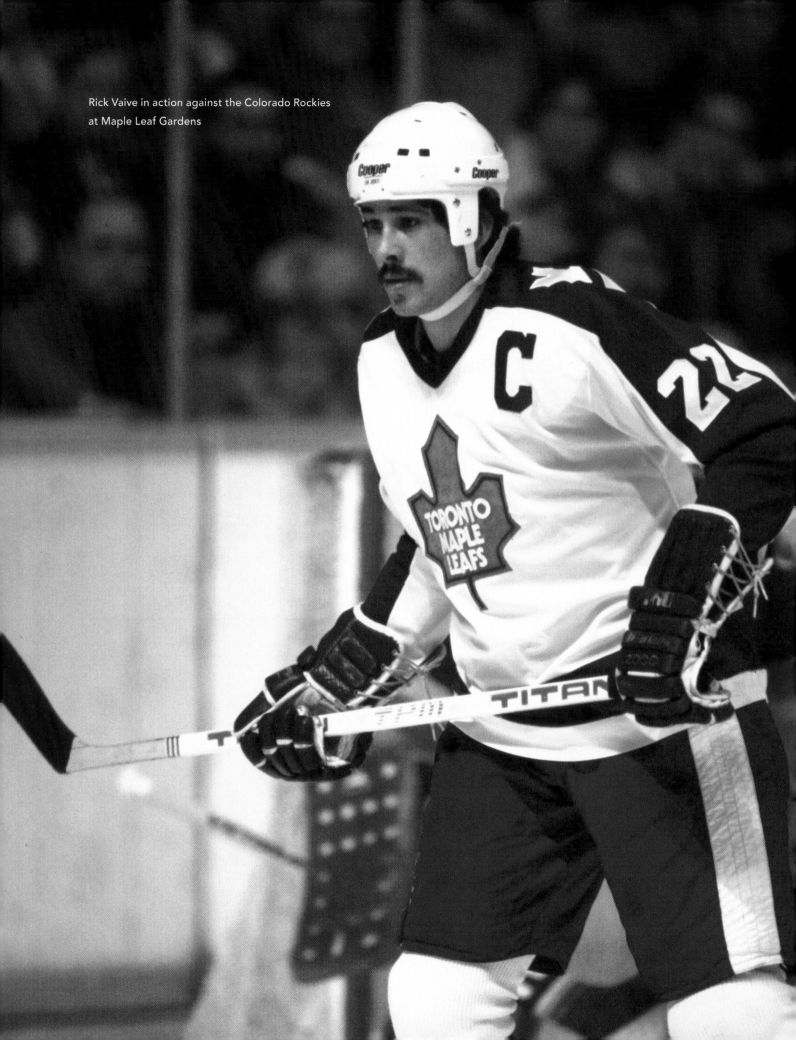

Rick Vaive in action against the Colorado Rockies
at Maple Leaf Gardens

RICK VAIVE

RIGHT WING • 1979–80 TO 1986–87 **C**

Born: **May 14, 1959, Ottawa, Ontario**
Games: **534** Goals: **299** Assists: **238** Points: **537** PIMs: **940**

Vaive was just 22 when he succeeded Darryl Sittler as Leafs captain. He was a straight-up wing gunner with a willingness to go to the net and a fear-inspiring arsenal of shots. A right-winger, he remains the only Maple Leaf to pile up three 50-goal seasons.

Vaive worked tirelessly to hone his release, and he used a massive stick that was a third heavier than that of his teammates. He nicknamed the stick "Big Bertha" and did a roaring trade.

In an era dominated by the finesse talents of Wayne Gretzky and Marcel Dionne, Rick Vaive was a pure gunner.

"I just can't see myself considered equal with the goalscoring abilities of players like Mike Bossy or Wayne Gretzky," he once said. "Watch how they score their goals. They come in on the net, make fancy moves and pick the corners.

"I just blast away."

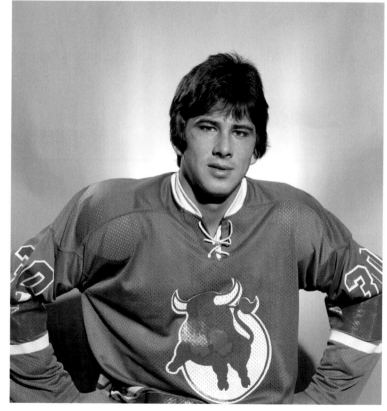

Rick Vaive as a member of the WHA's Birmingham Bulls

BILL DERLAGO

CENTRE • 1979–80 TO 1985–86

Born: **August 25, 1958, Birtle, Manitoba**
Games: **378** Goals: **158** Assists: **176** Points: **334** PIMs: **179**

Rick Vaive's three 50-goal seasons were due in a large part to Bill Derlago. Derlago was the author of Vaive's prodigious offence, the set-up man whose talent was jaw-dropping. Vaive's 50th in March 1982 came after Derlago stickhandled past two Blues and fed his right winger. A year later, Vaive's 50th came after Derlago cleanly won a faceoff and whipped the puck to his winger.

"Getting a pass from Bill Derlago," Vaive once said, "was a magical experience."

A better than average skater, Derlago had the instincts of the pure playmaker and the scoring gift of a gunner. Players who practised against him were often jarred by his gifts. As an 18-year-old with the Brandon Wheat Kings, Derlago scored 50 goals in just 27 games. Then 52 in 1989. He finished his junior career with a staggering 96-goal season.

Derlago posted four seasons of 30 goals as a Leaf, but he wanted no part of superstardom.

"The worst thing that can happen is getting 40 goals," Derlago once famously told a young player. "If you get 40, they want 45 or 50. Pretty soon you're in the coach's office every day."

Derlago might not have reached the 40-goal plateau, but his contribution and partnership with Vaive made him a valued Leaf and a part of this epic history.

BORJE SALMING

DEFENCE • 1973–74 TO 1988–89

Born: **April 17, 1951, Kiruna, Sweden**
Games: **1,099** Goals: **148** Assists: **620** Points: **768** PIMs: **1,292**
Inducted into Hockey Hall of Fame: **1996**

Borje Salming, the first Swede elected to the Hockey Hall of Fame, was a trailblazer for every European star who would shine in the NHL. As such, he bore countless scars. North American players, almost all of them Canadian, saw the game as theirs and the Europeans as interlopers bent on "stealing" jobs.

"It wasn't an easy time," Salming said later. "There were a lot of taunts of Chicken Swedes. There were threats to kill me. In Philadelphia, you had to stay away from the boards because they would try to grab you and yell at you."

"When you looked at Borje after a game there were welts and bruises and scars all over from guys trying to spear or run him," said Darryl Sittler. "Plus he was one of the best shot-blockers in the league."

Gifted with every talent that can be bestowed on a defenceman, Salming governed the Leafs blueline for 16 seasons. A two-time runner-up for the Norris Trophy as the league's best defenceman, he was a beautiful skater and a tremendous passer. While his status as the NHL's first great Swedish import made him a constant target for the goon tactics that often overran 1970s hockey, Salming usually gave as well as he got.

Only a player of unquestioned courage could have stood up to the abuse. Conn Smythe, a pillar of the hockey establishment, marvelled at Salming's determination. "That Swede is a courageous man with skill and

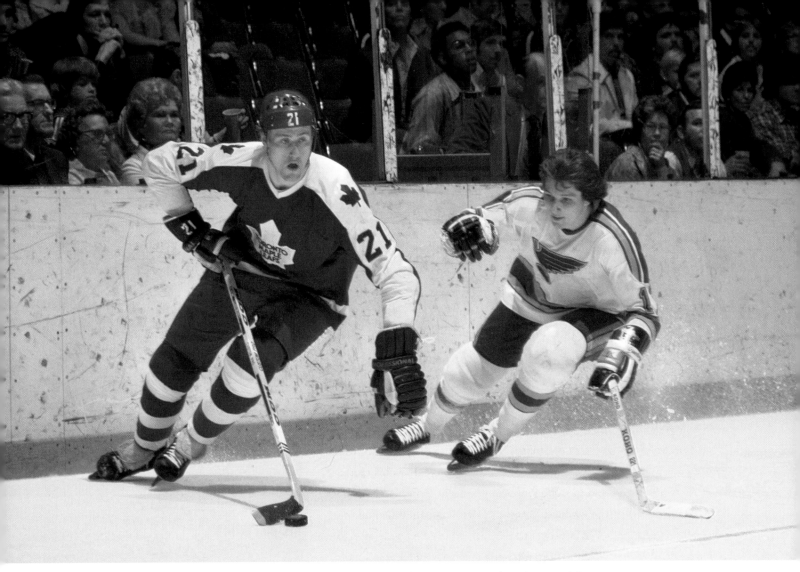

Borje Salming being chased by Jerry Butler, St. Louis Arena, March 15, 1977. Toronto beat St. Louis 4–1

guts who shows that hockey players are the cream of the crop all over the world," Smythe said.

Salming is the standardbearer among Leafs defenceman for goals, assists, and points. He was a first or second team all-star six times and his skill level often left his teammates dumbstruck.

"I remember watching Borje go into the corner with two guys right on him," said Leafs defenceman Bob McGill. "He would hold the guys off with one arm, put his foot on the puck, slide it backwards, pivot and lose the two checkers. He did things that nobody else could do."

In the middle of the 1970s, Philadelphia coach Fred Shero, whose teams had regularly tried to intimidate Salming, recognized the folly of the exercise during a playoff series with the Leafs.

"At the end of a long, heavy season, Salming played at least 35 to 40 minutes against us and in the third period he still was making dangerous rushes," Shero said. "He's a player of skill, stamina, and courage."

Perhaps the most expansive tribute to Salming's perseverance came on a night in 2006 when the Leafs honoured him and raised his number 21 to the rafters prior to a game against the Ottawa Senators. When Salming dropped the puck, it fell between Mats Sundin and Daniel Alfredsson, two Swedes who followed in the path Salming blazed.

VINCENT
DAMPHOUSSE

LEFT WING • 1986–87 TO 1990–91

Born: **December, 17, 1967, Montreal, Quebec**
Games: **394** Goals: **118** Assists: **211** Points: **329** PIMs: **362**

He was supposed to be a piano player. Growing up in Montreal, Vincent Damphousse was torn between two loyalties: his mother's love of music and the love for hockey Vincent shared with his dad.

"I loved music and I wanted Vincent to pay," Suzanne Damphousse recalls. "His father favoured hockey. I favoured music. His music teacher said he had a fine touch, that he might go far, but it needed a total commitment."

Damphousse chose hockey.

"It caused me a lot of tears and a lot of pain but it was for the best," Suzanne said.

Damphousse had the opportunity to play alongside a master. As a 15-year-old, he skated with Mario Lemieux on the Laval Voisins team on which Lemieux recorded 282 points. No surprise that Damphousse's fine 29-goal and 63-point campaign went somewhat unnoticed.

"We weren't friends or anything," Damphousse said, "but just playing with him showed me the possibilities. You may never be as good as Mario Lemieux, but he made you want to try."

Damphousse was the first-ever francophone Leaf drafted in the first round. The Leafs selected him sixth overall in 1986 and through five seasons with Toronto, Damphousse proved himself a gifted scorer with a willingness to deliver excellent defensive play. Damphousse recorded a 94-point season in 1989-90.

Vincent Damphousse and Lee Norwood of the Detroit Red Wings

Articulate but soft-spoken, Damphousse was much like his game: understated. Though he wasn't a dazzling playmaker, he was economical and prolific.

"He's right up there with the top scorers in the league and yet you don't really hear a lot about it," Wendel Clark once said. "I don't think he minds the lack of attention though. He loves the game. The other stuff might get in the way."

Though he was traded in 1991 for Grant Fuhr and Glenn Anderson, Damphousse would have been content to be a Maple Leaf forever. "I've never wanted to play anywhere else," he once said.

WENDEL CLARK

LEFT WING • 1985–86 TO 1993–94/1995–96 TO 1997–98/1999–00 C

Born: **October 25, 1966, Kelvington, Saskatchewan**
Games: **608** Goals: **260** Assists: **181** Points: **441** PIMs **1,535**

"I just wanted to be a hockey player," Wendel Clark said on the June day in 2000 that he retired. "That's pretty much the whole story."

No one doubted the first part of that statement. No one believed the second. Wendel Clark was the most devastating player to ever wear blue and white. Others could score more: Clark's 260 goals put him eighth all-time among Leafs players. Some, Tie Domi and Tiger Williams to name two, fought more. But there was no player whose total package of skills could match the impact Clark packed into his five-foot-ten, 200-pound frame.

Clark's rambunctious style took a toll on his body, and his career was beset by injuries. "I think that was a factor," said Leafs winger Steve Thomas, who first played with Clark in 1985–86. "He was 5-10 but played like he was 6-3. It showed the heart he had."

Clark spent 12-½ seasons over three stints in Toronto. He was a 30-plus goalscorer five times. The height of Clark's popularity probably came during the 1993 playoffs, when he and Doug Gilmour carried an

Wendel Clark battles Detroit Red Wings defenceman Vladimir Konstantinov
and goalie Tim Cheveldae

overachieving team to the semi-finals. The following year he scored a career-best 46 goals in only 64 games. Sensing he had an asset that was at the height of its value, Cliff Fletcher swapped Clark to Quebec in a deal that brought Mats Sundin to Toronto.

In 2000, Clark came back for a final 20 games plus six playoff contests. If the goals came more sparingly, the hits did not. In a memorable regular season finale, Clark repeatedly threw himself into the New Jersey Devils. If the Zamboni driver had shown up on the ice, Wendel Clark would have hit him too.

At 33, there was nothing left. "My body was done," Clark would later say. "If I even looked at my equipment I hurt for three days."

He was beloved by Leafs fans, which made his retirement in Toronto fitting, even though Clark also played in Quebec, Long Island, Tampa, Detroit, and Chicago.

"I started as a Leaf and I can end as a Leaf," he said. "No matter where I played, this always felt like home."

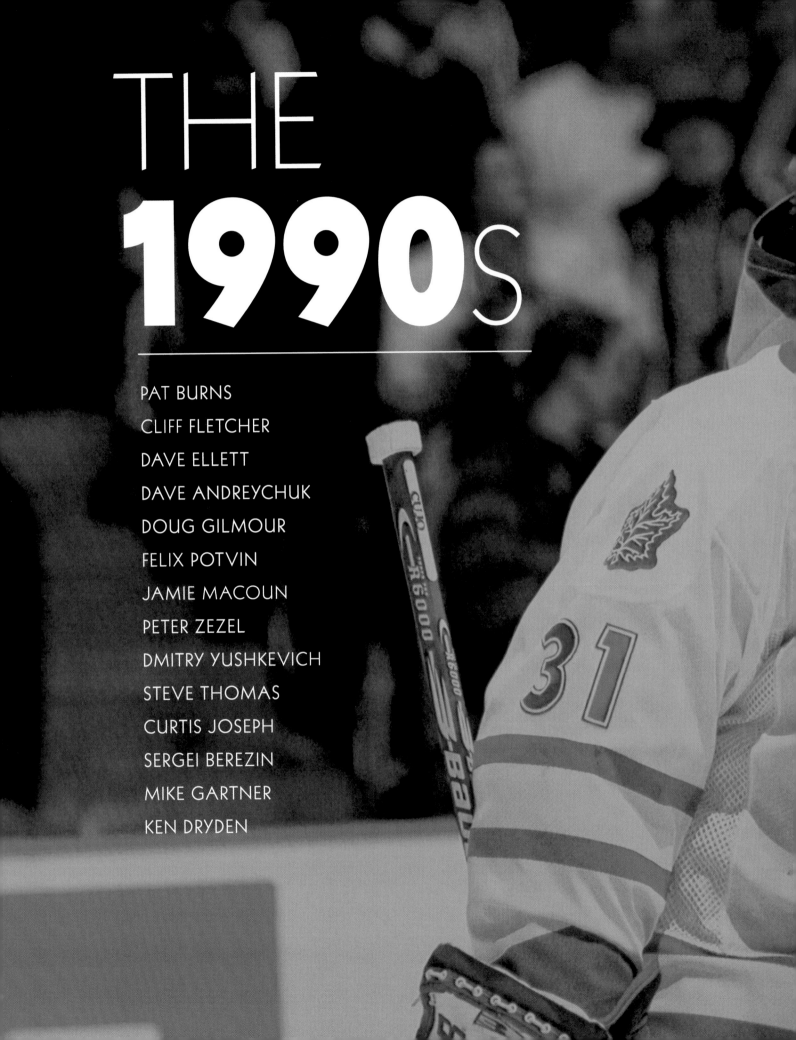

THE
1990s

PAT BURNS

CLIFF FLETCHER

DAVE ELLETT

DAVE ANDREYCHUK

DOUG GILMOUR

FELIX POTVIN

JAMIE MACOUN

PETER ZEZEL

DMITRY YUSHKEVICH

STEVE THOMAS

CURTIS JOSEPH

SERGEI BEREZIN

MIKE GARTNER

KEN DRYDEN

Curtis Joseph and Bryan Berard

TEAM OF THE DECADE
1992–93 TORONTO MAPLE LEAFS

REGULAR SEASON RECORD: 32-42-6
PLAYOFF RECORD: 7-6

The renaissance of the Leafs franchise, atrophied during the Harold Ballard years, began in 1992. The architect was Cliff Fletcher. The foreman was coach Pat Burns. The lead hand was Doug Gilmour.

The Leafs jumped 22 points in Burns's first season with the club as Gilmour recorded a career-high 127 points. Dave Andreychuk, acquired by Fletcher in a deal that sent Grant Fuhr to Buffalo, poured in 25 goals in just 31 regular season games and then 12 more in 21 playoff contests. In one season, Burns lifted the Leafs from 12th to second in team defence. Felix Potvin led the league in GAA with a 2.50 aggregate.

Wendel Clark shrugged off an injury-plagued season with 10 post-season goals and 20 playoff points in 21 games as the Leafs upset Detroit in 7 games, downed a stubborn St. Louis team, and then finally fell in 7 games to Los Angeles. Wayne Gretzky scored a hat trick in Game 7 to spoil what would have been a dream final – a 1967 rematch between the Leafs and the Canadiens. Still, the team's first appearance in the third round in 15 years put the league on notice – the Leafs were back.

PAT BURNS

COACH • 1992–96

Born: **April 4, 1952, Montreal, Quebec** Died: **November 19, 2010 (58), Sherbrooke, Quebec**
Games: **281** Record: **133 W, 107 L, 41 T** Pts. %: **.546**
Awards: **Jack Adams Award, 1993**
Inducted into Hockey Hall of Fame: **2014 (Builder)**

The first change was about housekeeping. When Pat Burns arrived to guide the Maple Leafs in 1992, one of his premier edicts was that no sweater would ever touch the ground.

"After a game," said Mike Foligno, one of the scores of journeymen who found a spot as a Burns footsoldier, "we used to throw our sweaters into a shopping cart in the middle of the dressing room to be laundered."

If some of the jerseys missed the target, a trainer or equipment manager would pick it up soon enough. That was not good enough for Pat Burns.

"Pat wanted to make sure we held ourselves accountable for the fact that we were playing in a hockey-hungry city like Toronto," Foligno said. "I remember him saying he was so proud to be able to coach an Original Six team, and he wanted to impress upon us what that meant."

From day one, the sweater would become a symbol to be treated with respect. Under Burns, the name on the front meant more than the name on the back.

Pat Burns fuelled his teams with anger. Burns had been a police officer in Gatineau, Quebec, for 16 years, and he was cop to the core. He could smell the lie behind a lack of effort, and he meted out discipline unyieldingly.

Pat Burns with his Jack Adams Award, which he won three times in his career

"Burnsie was a hard-ass," said Wendel Clark, who captained the Leafs under Burns for two seasons. "In a lot of ways he made the team pull together to spite him. We didn't always love Burnsie the morning after games after what he did to us the night before, but we all respected the direction the team was going."

When Burns arrived, the Leafs hadn't had a winning team since 1976–77, and he was relentless in demanding a new level of performance. Once, in his first season with the Leafs, Burns convened his post-game press conference in the middle of the dressing room in Detroit rather than in an adjacent hallway or media room. He savaged the performance of the team as the players dressed a few feet away.

"He was a big man and he could be very intimidating," said Doug Gilmour. "Actually, he would scare the crap out of us. The funny thing about Burnsie is he hated complacency. If we were on a winning streak he made us practise harder than if we weren't going good. If we lost a few, he would give us more time off to recover."

The Leafs would rack up 99 points in that first season, and Gilmour, a model of competitiveness to begin with, enjoyed his best seasons under Burns's often-withering glare.

But no coach could ask what Pat Burns asked for indefinitely. "Pat was the type of coach who would never have a long tenure in one place because he was so demanding and got so much out of his players," said his GM Cliff Fletcher. "After a number of years, if he had that same group of players, they just collapsed. They had no more to give."

The team's seven-game defeat in the semi-finals to Wayne Gretzky and the Los Angeles Kings in 1992 would rank among his greatest disappointments. He would win his only Stanley Cup in New Jersey in 2003.

A few months before Burns's death at the age of 58, his former players packed a suite at the Air Canada Centre, closed the door to the world, and welcomed and roasted Burns in a wash of beer and love. For most of them that was goodbye.

"Deep down we knew he loved us," Doug Gilmour said. "And deep down … we adored him."

CLIFF
FLETCHER

GENERAL MANAGER • 1991–97 AND 1998

Born: **August 16, 1935, Montreal, Quebec**
Games: **493** Record: **219 W, 213 L, 58 T, 3 OTL** Pts. %: **.506**
Inducted into Hockey Hall of Fame: **2004 (Builder)**

Cliff Fletcher, 2012

C liff Fletcher's career began with a $200-a-year salary from the Montreal Canadiens and a team jacket to seal the deal. A Hall of Fame builder, Fletcher's legacy to the Maple Leafs includes the acquisition of two Hall of Fame players: Doug Gilmour and Mats Sundin.

There are no more Cliff Fletchers; the NHL salary cap has complicated player trades to the point that mega deals like the ones Fletcher specialized in are no longer feasible.

Fletcher spent a decade in Montreal under the tutelage of the Canadiens' legendary general manager, Sam Pollock, who stressed the importance of scouting and the art of a complicated deal.

Fletcher managed the Atlanta Flames, helped smooth the team's move to Calgary, and won a Cup in 1989. Twice Fletcher's teams had the best record in the league, but the presence of the dynastic Edmonton Oilers kept Fletcher's Cup total to one.

Fletcher took over the Maple Leafs in 1991 and ran the team for six years. In 2008, he rejoined the club, stepping in as acting GM, and then handed the reins to Brian Burke to assume the role of senior adviser and statesman. When he arrived in Toronto, Fletcher began by restoring pride in the logo. He welcomed alumni, unwanted in the Harold Ballard years, back into the fold. He made 51 trades, better than eight a year, in his first stint with the team.

Fletcher's strength was his ability to understand the needs of the GM with whom he was working. "My philosophy is to put yourself in the other GM's shoes," Fletcher said. "It starts with trying to understand whether he thinks it's a good fit or not."

"Right from the time you're a kid, any aspiring GM wants to work in Montreal or Toronto," Fletcher once said. "I consider it fulfilling a lifelong dream to have started with the Canadiens and ended my career with the Leafs."

DAVE
ELLETT

DEFENCE • 1990–91 TO 1996–97

Born: **March 30, 1964, Cleveland, Ohio**
Games: **446** Goals: **51** Assists: **172** Points: **223** PIMs: **371**

Dave Ellett's hockey bloodlines meant he was a seasoned traveler at an early age. His family frequented Port Arthur, Ottawa, Cleveland, Houston, Salt Lake City, Seattle, and Rochester – the minor league stops undertaken by his father, Bob, who played in the days of the six-team league. As the son of a minor league journeyman, Ellett understood the life of the hockey pro from the beginning.

"Yeah, we put a few miles on every year going to a new city, but we met a lot of friends and went to a lot of schools," Ellett said. "The toughest part was the new school every year, but I really liked hanging around the different rinks."

Ellett was a Winnipeg Jets draft pick who learned the trade from a pack of veteran blueliners that included Randy Carlyle. His three-year $2.1 million-contract with the Leafs in 1991 was the highest accorded in the club's history. Ellett's offensive production with the Leafs peaked with an 18-goal, 51-point season in 1992, but he thrived as a key member of a defensive corps that included Sylvain Lefebvre, Jamie Macoun, Todd Gill, and Bob Rouse. When the Leafs roared into the playoffs under Pat Burns in 1992, the group were a combined plus 41 in the regular season and plus 24 in the playoffs.

Dave Ellett was an accomplished NHL defenceman who played 1,129 NHL games. He used the instincts he had honed as a kid watching his dad to always be a little ahead of the play.

"I try to play the game with my head and anticipate things," Ellett once said. "If you can anticipate, you don't spend your whole night having to win one-on-one battles."

DAVE
ANDREYCHUK

LEFT WING • 1992–93 TO 1995–96

Born: **September 29, 1963, Hamilton, Ontario**
Games: **223** Goals: **120** Assists: **99** Points: **219** PIMs: **194**

Dave Andreychuk was six foot four with a reach so long it has been said that he made bending over while tying his skates optional. There was also the matter of his hands — as skilled as any safecracker's. Those two elements made Andreychuck's pokey skating skills largely irrelevant.

From the moment Cliff Fletcher acquired Andreychuk in a deal that sent eventual Hall of Fame goalie Grant Fuhr to Buffalo, Andreychuk was the perfect foil for his centreman Doug Gilmour. Traded at Christmastime in 1992, Andreychuk scored 25 goals in 31 Leafs games to finish the season with a combined 54, the highest total ever for a Leaf.

Andreychuk was an instant favourite of Pat Burns, who used him in all situations, including the penalty kill, and Andreychuk rewarded Burns with a Leafs record 12-goal playoff run in the 1993 post-season. The run helped bury a reputation of falling short in the playoffs.

"He doesn't get the respect he deserves," Gilmour once said. "He's done everything for us."

That lack of attention never bothered the easygoing Andreychuk. "Goalscoring never came easy to me," he said. "Just because you have a little bit of talent doesn't mean you will score. A lot of it is guessing, realizing where the puck is going to go and most of the times you're wrong. When you're right, people say it was easy."

The Stanley Cup that eluded Andreychuk in Toronto would find him captaining Tampa as a 40-year-old. No player waited longer than the 1,597 regular season and 162 playoff games it took for Andreychuk to hit paydirt.

93 DOUG GILMOUR

C CENTRE • 1991–92 TO 1996–97/2002–03

Born: **June 25, 1963, Kingston, Ontario**
Games: **393** Goals: **131** Assists: **321** Points: **452** PIMs: **386**
Awards: **Frank Selke Trophy, 1993**
Inducted into Hockey Hall of Fame: **2011**

Doug Gilmour played only 393 regular season games as a Maple Leaf. That's fewer than players such as Dave Ellett (446 games) and Dan Daoust (518). Yet Gilmour remains one of the most beloved figures in the team's history. Many would put him at the top of the list. That's because no player's desire for success was as transparent, and was recognized and understood as readily and completely, as Doug Gilmour's.

Chicken-chested and just five foot nine, Gilmour battled bigger men all his life. As a junior, Gilmour became expert at stashing weights in his sweats and mastered subtly standing on his tiptoes during weigh ins. Drafted in the seventh round by the St. Louis Blues in 1982, Gilmour converted every slight into defiance. He bled, literally and often, for and on his jersey, and in the playoffs, he seemed to grow more dog-eared with each period.

He invaded scrums he should have avoided and traded slashes at the slightest provocation. "If they outlawed fighting in the NHL," he once cracked, "I'd lead the league in penalties every year."

Gilmour was the centrepiece of one of Cliff Fletcher's most brilliant trades, a 10-player swap that ended a contract impasse between Gilmour and the Calgary Flames. Accepting the captaincy from another famed tough guy, Red Horner, seemed predestined.

"It's almost like Doug has been training for a role like this his whole life," Fletcher said.

Doug Gilmour faces off against Peter Stastny of the St. Louis Blues

Gilmour hit Toronto at the very peak of his production. It was the perfect role at the perfect time: coach Pat Burns revered Gilmour's incendiary competitiveness, and Gilmour was soon to be flanked by Dave Andreychuk, who complemented him well with his giant's reach and surgeon's touch.

Gilmour led the Leafs to two final-four appearances and produced post-season points by the bushel. His 77 points in just 52 games remains the Leafs record. During one of his Leafs playoff runs, Pat Burns was asked if Gilmour had been given a day off.

"Dougie's gone back to his home planet," Burns said.

Gilmour would play for the New Jersey Devils, Chicago Blackhawks, Buffalo Sabres, and the Montreal Canadiens before he was traded to the Leafs for one final stint in 2003. A knee injury suffered in the first period of his first game back ended his career. The reunion with Toronto fans would never come.

When inducted into the Hockey Hall of Fame in 2011, Gilmour said: "To the people who said I was too small, that I'd never have a chance, I'd like to say thank you because if it wasn't for them, I wouldn't have worked as hard as I did."

Doug Gilmour celebrating a goal against the Vancouver Canucks

FELIX POTVIN

GOALTENDER • 1991–92 TO 1998–99

Born: **June 23, 1971, Anjou, Quebec**
Games: **369** Wins: **160** Losses: **149** Ties: **49** Shutouts: **12** Goals against: **2.87**

They called him the "Cat," but Felix Potvin was more of a workhorse. For six full seasons and part of two more, Potvin was the backstop for competitive Leafs teams, including two outfits that advanced to the third round of the NHL playoffs.

Potvin burst onto the scene in 1992–93 and supplanted Hall of Fame goalie Grant Fuhr. Coach Pat Burns went with Potvin against heavily favoured Detroit in the first round. Potvin was torched for six goals in each of his first two games, but Burns stuck with him.

"I don't blame Potvin for nothing," Burns said, and he was speaking for the group.

That decision was one of the early markers for Potvin's career. "The fact that I had given up 12 goals in the first two games didn't bother me, because it didn't bother anyone else on the team," Potvin said. "They had confidence in me."

Potvin would eventually backstop the Leafs to a seven-game win over the Red Wings in what was the signature win of the Burns era. He played in the All-Star Game the following year, and in the playoffs posted three 1–0 shutouts in a first-round victory over Chicago. Potvin again lifted the Leafs into the third round, but the team fell to Vancouver.

Age and a crumbling defensive corps would eventually undo the Leafs. Potvin would post several good, but not great, seasons and was eventually traded to the Islanders in the deal that brought Bryan Berard to Toronto. He would also play for Vancouver, Los Angeles, and Boston before retiring at 32, but his impact would be long felt with the Leafs.

Among Leafs goalies, only Turk Broda (629 games) and Johnny Bower (472) played more regular season games than Felix Potvin (369), and his 160 Leafs victories put him third in wins behind Broda (302) and Bower (220).

JAMIE MACOUN

DEFENCE • 1991-92 TO 1997-98

Born: **August 17, 1961, Hamilton, Ontario**
Games: **466** Goals: **13** Assists: **88** Points: **101** PIMs: **506**

For six years, Jamie Macoun patrolled the Maple Leafs blueline with minimal publicity and maximum effectiveness. Macoun was part of the 10-player trade that brought Doug Gilmour to the Leafs in 1992. In 466 games he scored just 13 goals, but along with Dave Ellett, Macoun gave the Leafs a dependable pairing that could be counted on to snuff out the opposition's top-scoring units.

"What I do is not very glamorous," Macoun once said. "I don't get a chance to get a lot of points, but I think the people I play with appreciate me."

Macoun's road to the Leafs was a wandering one. He was undrafted into major junior because he stood only five feet tall on his 16th birthday. Macoun made himself into an excellent skater, but falling out of the development cycle meant no NHL team would gamble on him. Macoun instead attended Ohio State University on a hockey scholarship, quickly grew to six feet, two inches tall and suddenly found himself in demand.

He signed with the Calgary Flames after a little more than two years in the NCAA. His career took another turn in 1987 when he was seriously injured in a car accident that left doctors wondering if he would ever regain full use of his arm. After a season on the sidelines, Macoun returned and helped the Flames to their only Stanley Cup in 1999.

After Toronto, Macoun spent two seasons with Detroit. That stint resulted in his second Cup in 1998.

He would finish with 1,128 NHL games to his credit and a legacy as a key contributor to the two teams coached by Pat Burns that advanced to the third round of the playoffs.

PETER ZEZEL

CENTRE • 1990–91 TO 1993–94

Born: **April 22, 1965, Toronto, Ontario** Died: **May 26, 2009 (44), Toronto, Ontario**
Games: **207** Goals: **50** Assists: **78** Points: **128** PIMs: **73**

When Peter Zezel died, just 44, of a rare blood disease named hemolytic anemia, Leafs Nation lost a member of the team's most beloved checking line. The trio of Zezel, Mark Osborne, and Bill Berg was assembled and deployed by coach Pat Burns in 1993. The nucleus of the line was Zezel, a player who managed the transition from big-time scorer in junior and his early years as an NHLer to a faceoff expert and defensive stopper. He was also one of the most beloved Leafs.

"What we lost in Peter was a really special, special human being," Osborne said. "He was someone who mixed with everyone, from players to fans and everyone in between."

Zezel dressed for 15 seasons and 873 NHL games with Philadelphia, St. Louis, Washington, the Leafs, Dallas, New Jersey, and Vancouver. While he turned in excellent NHL scoring figures — 219 goals and 608 points, including a career high 33 goals and 79 points in Philadelphia — Zezel saw the faceoff circle as his office.

An excellent soccer player, Zezel was built like an

oversized fire hydrant. His low centre of gravity and wide-track build meant winning a faceoff was as simple as tying up an opponent's hands and directing the puck through his superior footwork.

"It's a matter of timing but my experience in soccer is a big help," Zezel once said. "You know, neutralize the other guy's stick and kick the puck to one of our players. Another thing is I have a low centre of gravity and that means I can sort of get under the player opposite me."

"Anytime you had a key faceoff in your end late in the game and you were protecting the lead he'd go out and get the job done for you," said Cliff Fletcher, who landed Zezel from Washington for Bob Rouse and Al Iafrate in 1991.

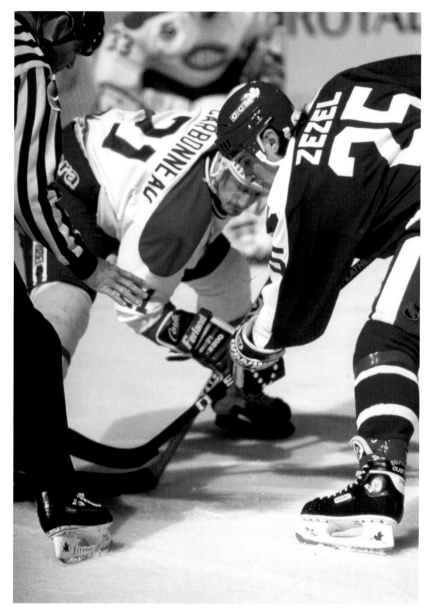

Peter Zezel faces off against Guy Carbonneau of the Montreal Canadiens

Zezel could still do damage offensively – he hit double figures in scoring three times as a Leaf – but he never complained about trading in the glamour of goalscoring for the grunt work in the circle.

"Sure, my goals and points went down but that's not what's expected of me now," he said. "My role is to play against the best centremen in the league and try to shut them down. I enjoy the challenge."

After his retirement, Zezel spent his time as a volunteer coach, fittingly for both soccer and hockey players.

"He was just a great guy, smiling all the time," remembered Fletcher. "It figured that he would be coaching. Peter Zezel was the kind of guy you wanted to coach your kid."

DMITRY
YUSHKEVICH

DEFENCE • 1995–96 TO 2001–02

Born: **November 19, 1971, Cherepovets, Soviet Union**
Games: **506** Goals: **25** Assists: **110** Points: **136** PIMs: **409**

Dmitry Yushkevich had a habit that used to drive his coach, Pat Quinn, to distraction. Like a basketball player taking a charge, Yushkevich compulsively positioned himself in front of the opposition's hardest-charging player. "I would say, 'Yushky, you don't have to do that.' But he'd say, 'Coach, I own that ice,'" Quinn recalled.

"He's probably the best open-ice hitter since Bob Baun," said another Leafs coach, Pat Burns.

Leafs forward Ken Baumgartner, a fearsome hitter himself, said your feelings about Yushkevich were determined by the colour of the sweater you wore. "There are only two ways at looking at Yushky's game," Baumgartner said. "You either appreciate it or you fear it."

Yushkevich took a winding road to the NHL. He grew up in a steel town 12 hours north of Moscow. He didn't go to his first hockey game until he was nine and didn't skate until he was 11.

Nothing speaks to Yushkevich's unpredictable nature better than his choice of a childhood role model.

From left: Igor Korolev, Dmitry Yushkevich, Jonas Hoglund, and Bryan McCabe

"My idol was Johnny Bower," he once said. "I wanted to be a goalie, but the coach saw that I was a good skater. He put someone who couldn't skate in net."

His affinity for playing goal can be seen in his style of play. On some nights Yushkevich seemed to block as many shots as the goalie behind him.

Yushkevich regularly played more than 25 minutes for Quinn, often paired with another Russian, Danny Markov. He never stopped punishing opposing players, even as the mountain of injuries to his feet, legs, face, and shoulders piled up.

"I do on the ice what you have to do to win. Sometimes it's putting your body in front of a puck, sometimes it's crushing a player. Whatever it takes," said Dmitry Yushkevich, "I do."

STEVE
THOMAS

32

Born: **July 15, 1963, Stockport, England**
Games: **377** Goals: **118** Assists: **173** Points: **291** PIMs: **299**

Steve Thomas didn't look like a goalscorer, at least until he had the puck on his stick. He was short, five foot nine, a sprite among the redwood defencemen, but his stocky build complemented Thomas's primary asset: an indomitable will to find the net.

"Steve was one of the toughest guys in the league," said Wendel Clark. "He played big and played hard. He was truly a competitor."

Thomas was never drafted as a junior but ripped through junior hockey and the AHL as a prolific scorer. Thomas scored 51 goals and added 54 assists with the Marlies in 1983–84. He scored 42 goals and added 48 assists in 64 AHL games with St. Catharines and was rookie of the year.

He did so largely on the strength of a terrific shot.

"I missed nine weeks of hockey once because of Stevie Thomas," said goalie Glenn Healey. "They had to dig the tip of my finger out of my blocker glove. His skill, his ability to create offence off the forecheck, recognizing situations and seizing them, it was all there with Steve Thomas."

Thomas was born in England but grew up a Leafs fan in Toronto. He bucked the odds and preconceptions on his size to carve out an excellent career.

"I was always proud to wear the Leaf," Thomas once said. "Every time I wore the uniform it was special."

Steve Thomas and Ray Bourque of the Boston Bruins

CURTIS
JOSEPH

GOALTENDER • 1998–99 TO 2001–02/2008–09

Born: **April 29, 1967, Keswick, Ontario**
Games: **270** Wins: **138** Losses: **97** Ties: **28** Shutouts: **17** Goals against: **2.49**
Awards: **King Clancy Award, 2000**

Curtis Joseph was hero, a goalie who shone most dramatically when his team was being outplayed. He was the mainstay of Leafs teams that twice advanced to the Stanley Cup final four.

Never drafted at any level, he nonetheless starred in St. Louis and Edmonton before signing on with the Leafs as a free agent in 1998.

"Curtis played his best hockey when his team wasn't the favourite," assessed Wendel Clark. "He went to the semis twice and while those teams had Mats Sundin they weren't clubs that were full of talent. A small group of guys drove those teams, but the backbone was Curtis."

"Before he got here the Leafs were a team that was asleep offensively," said his coach, Pat Quinn. "Curtis gave us the courage, the confidence to attack."

"Curtis was a giver," said his longtime backup Glenn Healy. "Whether it was his box for kids from Sick Kids Hospital or the time he spent with ill children or the help he would give a teammate, he was a giver. That goes a long way in the respect you get from your teammates."

Joseph was a beloved figure as a Leaf. A Toronto product, every game was a homecoming. "One of the best parts of playing here," he once said, "is you can look in the stands and see friends, teachers, people you grew up with."

Curtis Joseph celebrates a win over the Philadelphia Flyers, April 1, 2009, at the Air Canada Centre

When he retired, only three goalies – Martin Brodeur, Patrick Roy, and Ed Belfour – had more wins. However, unlike Joseph, all three of those goalies had won at least one Stanley Cup. But there is little doubt that his teams would have lost far more games without Curtis Joseph in goal.

"When I look back at my career, I never would have dreamt it would take me where it did," he said.

SERGEI BEREZIN

LEFT WING • 1996–97 TO 2000–01

Born: **November 5, 1971, Voskresensk, Soviet Union**
Games: **357** Goals: **126** Assists: **94** Points: **220** PIMs: **34**

Some called Sergei Berezin "The Rushin' Russian," and it was an article of faith among Leafs fans that Berezin shot no more often than he breathed. Berezin loved rushing the puck, loved shooting the puck, loved … no, that was about it. Pat Quinn once described a rush that resulted in a Berezin goal as "no, no, no, no … yes."

Assistant coach Alpo Suhonen, in defending Berezin's proclivity to shoot, put it perfectly: "He's not selfish. He's himself."

Berezin chafed when asked if he should pass more and shoot less.

"It's never too much," he said. "I don't take stupid shots from far away. Every shot I take is a scoring chance. If I take a shot it's because I think I can put it into the net."

There have been many worse ideas. Berezin was an excellent shooter, a finisher whose abundant skating skills often put him in alone on opposing netminders. Clearly, though, he thought he had more chances than he really had. He had more assists than goals in four of his five Leafs seasons.

Darryl Sittler and Player of the Game Sergei Berezin

Sergei Berezin shoots past Grant Ledyard of the Ottawa Senators

"Russian-trained wingers are attack people," reasoned Leafs coach Quinn. "They attack and shoot first and pass the puck later."

Nor was Berezin enamoured of the defensive elements of the job.

The left winger stayed true to a report compiled by Leafs scout Nick Beverley, who found Berezin playing in a German pro league. "When he sees an offensive chance, he has unlimited energy," Beverley said. "When the puck goes the other way, his legs get a bit heavy."

Berezin scored an average of 25 goals a year and distinguished himself as a fixture on the second power-play unit. One-quarter of Berezin's goals, including the series winner in the last minute of play to eliminate the Flyers in 1999, came with a man advantage.

For Berezin, shooting was an act of personal responsibility. "I play the way I live," he once said. "I always take charge of my life without trying to put it on somebody else's shoulders."

MIKE GARTNER

RIGHT WING • 1993–94 TO 1995–96

Born: **October 29, 1959, Ottawa, Ontario**
Games: **130** Goals: **53** Assists: **33** Points: **86** PIMs: **62**
Inducted into Hockey Hall of Fame: **2001**

W hat Mike Gartner achieved was the most impressive of unofficial records: in 1996, at the age of 36, Gartner wheeled around the Boston Garden ice in 13.375 seconds, the fastest an NHL player had managed to traverse the distance.

Gartner captured the fastest skating competition all three times he contested the All-Star event. Inconceivably fast, his All-Star dashes outdistanced players 10 or 15 years his junior. Gartner was also extraordinarily consistent. His 15 seasons of 30 or more goals remains a record. Among right wingers only Gordie Howe and Brett Hull scored more goals than Gartner.

The goals were built on speed in attacking the zone – a speed Gartner amply displayed in 1994–95 and 1995–96, when he scored 53 goals in 130 Leafs games.

Figure skating consultant and former world champion Barb Underhill, who mentored dozens of Leafs on ways to improve their skating, considered Gartner the perfect skater among hockey players.

"If you watch Mike, you see his skate lands on the exact ideal location for speed and efficiency. He has the closest thing I have seen among hockey players to a perfect skating stride."

Gartner always credited the instruction he received as a child for his skating ability. "It's a natural gift to a degree," he said, "but if you've been

Mike Gartner looking for a scoring opportunity against Rick Tabaracci of the Calgary Flames

Gartner and Grant Ledyard of the Dallas Stars

taught correctly to skate economically, you don't waste your energy and get the most out of what God gave you."

Despite a Hall of Fame career, the one place Gartner's blades were never able to carry him was hockey's ultimate winner's circle. He did not win a Stanley Cup but was voted to the Hall of Fame by virtue of a remarkable offensive productivity that resulted in 708 goals and 1,338 points over 1,433 NHL regular season games.

KEN
DRYDEN

PRESIDENT 1997–99

Born: **August 8, 1947, Hamilton, Ontario**
Games: **164** Record: **75 W, 73 L, 16 OTL** Pts. %: **.506**
Inducted into Hockey Hall of Fame: **1983**

K en Dryden, goalie, politician, author, and lawyer, ushered the Maple Leafs from their historic home, Maple Leaf Gardens, to the Air Canada Centre, moving the team from a hallowed but limited venue into one of the finest facilities in the NHL.

Hired in May 1997 to be the president of the Leafs, Dryden's search for a GM ended on his own doorstep. The Leafs were a .500 team during his two-year tenure as GM, but it should come as no surprise that Dryden's biggest impact was in goaltending.

It was Dryden who signed Curtis Joseph to a free-agent contract in 1998. He also signed free agent Steve Thomas, who would enjoy several productive years flanking superstar centre Mats Sundin.

While he would leave the Leafs for a career in politics after seven years with the team, Dryden's reputation as a winner lent credibility and a winning pedigree to the franchise.

"It's a very stimulating and varied job," he once said. "The interesting discovery for me is that it's a lot like what you do with your own kids. Try to make them better. Try to help them out. That's the puzzle, the challenge, and the wonderful part."

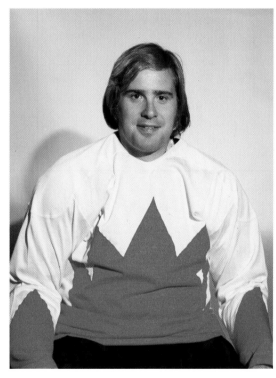

Ken Dryden, Team Canada, 1972

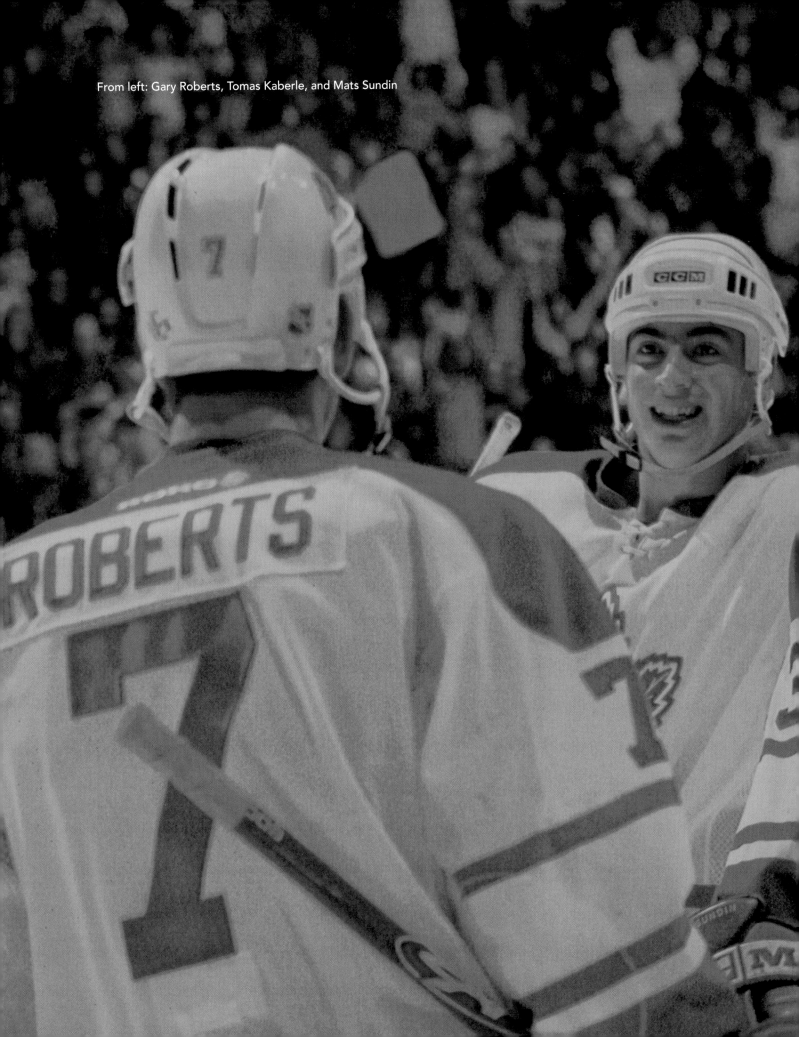

From left: Gary Roberts, Tomas Kaberle, and Mats Sundin

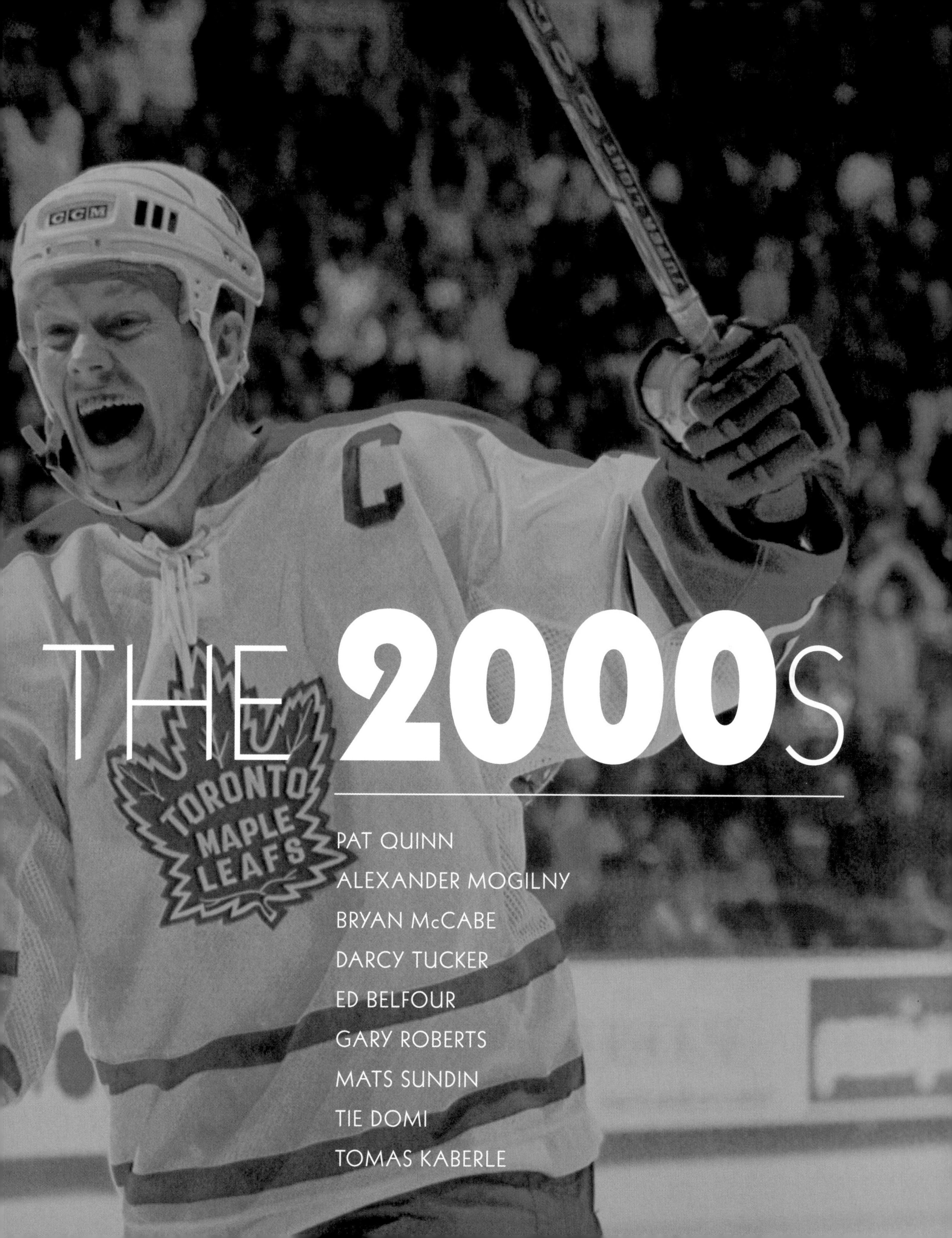

THE 2000s

TORONTO MAPLE LEAFS

PAT QUINN

ALEXANDER MOGILNY

BRYAN McCABE

DARCY TUCKER

ED BELFOUR

GARY ROBERTS

MATS SUNDIN

TIE DOMI

TOMAS KABERLE

TEAM OF THE DECADE
2001–02 TORONTO MAPLE LEAFS

REGULAR SEASON RECORD: 43-25-10
PLAYOFF RECORD: 10-10

The franchise's first 100-point team, the 2001–02 Leafs were a high-octane unit that finished second in the league in offence and rode a terrific season from goalie Curtis Joseph (.906 save percentage, and a 2.23 goals against average), who emboldened the Leafs from the crease on out. The club boasted an excellent group of forwards led by Mats Sundin (41 goals), Darcy Tucker, and Alexander Mogilny (24 goals each). The team had grit in Tucker, Tie Domi, Wade Belak, and Dave Manson; offensively proficient defencemen in Bryan McCabe and Tomas Kaberle; a defensive hard rock in Dmitry Yushkevich; and a fleet of capable role players in Garry Valk, Travis Green, and Alyn McCauley.

When an injury limited Sundin to eight playoff games, the 35-year-old Roberts produced at a point-a-game clip and ended Game 2 against Ottawa with a goal in the third overtime period. Mogilny scored eight goals as the Maple Leafs ground out seven-game wins over the New York Islanders and Ottawa Senators before falling to Carolina in six games.

In the off-season, Joseph would bolt for Detroit after four years with the Leafs, and while Ed Belfour would prove an excellent replacement, the Leafs would not return to the third round.

23

PAT QUINN

DEFENCE • 1968–69 TO 1969–70
COACH • 1998–2006
GENERAL MANAGER • 1999–2003

Born: **January 29, 1943, Hamilton, Ontario**
Games (player): **99** Goals: **2** Assists: **12** Points: **14** PIMs: **183**
Games (coach): **574** Record: **300 W, 196 L, 52 T, 26 OTL** Pts. %: **.591**

Quinn started his career as a journeyman player who squeezed the most out of his modest skills: 606 NHL games, including 99 on the Leafs' blueline. As a coach, he favoured skill over brawn, advocated for European players before it was popular, and carved out a role as a cigar-smoking philosopher-coach.

Bigger than life, he traded on the image he created, even after health issues mandated a slimmer profile and abstinence from tobacco.

"To be successful you have to drum up emotion," he said. "I want to be a combination motivator, teacher, mentor, and coach."

He could be frightfully intimidating.

"When I was an assistant for Pat in Vancouver, he came into the dressing room one time and went wild," said former Leafs coach Ron Wilson. "I don't know about the players, but he scared the crap out of

Pat Quinn holds back the Boston Bruins

me. He cussed and swore. After he was done, we went back into his office and he asked us: 'Do you think they bought it?'"

At 63, after his only Leafs season outside the playoffs in eight tries, Quinn was fired by John Ferguson Jr., who sensed that the team needed a change behind the bench. Quinn's 300 wins and 574 games as coach were bettered only by Punch Imlach, for whom Quinn played in his two seasons as a Leaf. His winning percentage of .591 was the best in franchise history.

"Pat played the game, he knows what you feel," defenceman Tomas Kaberle once said. "When I got tired late in my first year, he put me in the press box but it wasn't punishment. He said, 'It's okay, watch and rest.' He told me not to get down, to keep my head up. That was a very important message for a young guy."

Relentless in his quest to improve and to learn, Quinn charted a unique career. He made himself into a player when it would have paid about as much to be a goon. He made himself into a lawyer when it would have been enough to be a hockey player. Then he made himself into a coach when it would have been enough to be a lawyer and a player.

"Pat Quinn is one of the greatest coaches of all time," said Wilson. "There's no one I respect in hockey more than Pat Quinn."

ALEXANDER
MOGILNY

RIGHT WING • 2001–02 TO 2003–04

Born: **February 18, 1969, Khabarovsk, Soviet Union**
Games: **176** Goals: **65** Assists: **101** Points: **166** PIMs: **32**
Awards: **Lady Byng Trophy, 2003**

His talent was limitless, and so many think that Alexander Mogilny's greatness was never fully realized. But Mogilny's 473 career goals and 1,032 points struck over 990 games speak to his brilliance.

He scored 166 points with the Maple Leafs over three seasons, but hip ailments conspired to limit his achievements.

"A lot of times he played when he was hurt, and even when he was, he had a big effect on your lineup," said former Leafs coach Pat Quinn. "He was a guy you could put anywhere. We could have put him on defence and he would have been great."

He was slightly built and seemed smaller in real life than he appeared on the ice, but with the puck on his stick and a few feet of ice to navigate Alexander Mogilny was astonishing.

"Alex is probably the most talented player I've played with in my entire career. That includes Joe Sakic and a lot of great players like Peter Forsberg," Mats Sundin once said. "In terms of sheer talent, he was the best."

Harvested from the small town of Khabarovsk in the eastern Soviet Union, Mogilny was the first member of the Soviet hockey factory to defect. He was 20, and there was no shortage of elements to rebel against, including the dour dictates of famed Soviet coach Viktor Tikhonov.

"I've always been making decisions different than what the others make," Mogilny once said. "I did what I wanted. I've always been that way since I was little. I always did what I wanted."

Leadership was never really part of that description. Mogilny never accepted the role of athlete as spokesman. He endured the media but hated the notion of explaining himself to anyone.

"I'm not a star athlete," he once told a writer. "You say I'm a star athlete. I'm not anything. I'm a hockey player. That's what I was from the beginning – a hockey player, even when I was playing for nothing. To me, it isn't anyone's business how my head feels or how my stomach feels or if my little finger is okay."

True to form, Mogilny surprised when asked about playing in the fishbowl that is Toronto. The team's sophisticated fan base accepted Mogilny. Genius was to be admired.

"My family and I really enjoyed it in Toronto," he said. "We had a great experience. I can't say enough about how great the fans were to me. I really appreciated it."

BRYAN McCABE

DEFENCE • 2000–01 TO 2007–08

Born: **June 8, 1975, St. Catharines, Ontario**
Games: **523** Goals: **83** Assists: **214** Points: **297** PIMs: **785**

Bryan McCabe and Mark Parrish of the New York Islanders

Bryan McCabe invariably greeted the good and bad of being a Maple Leaf with the same good-natured grin.

"You definitely have to be a specific type of player to survive and succeed in Toronto," he once said. "You are always in a pressure-type situation. You are recognized on the ice, going to the store. If you can handle it, it's great. If you can't, it can be tough."

McCabe was a formidable talent willing to block shots and manhandle opponents in the corner. Blessed with one of the hardest shots in the league, he was named to the NHL's second all-star team and enjoyed 15-, 16-, 17-, and 19-goal seasons with the Leafs. He was an alternate for Team Canada at the 2006 Olympics.

"I think McCabe can win the Norris Trophy," said Hall of Famer Brian Leetch who played 15 regular season games with Berard in 2004. "He's the best player I've played with in my career as a partner."

The Leafs acquired McCabe from the Chicago Blackhawks for Alexander Karpovtsev and a pair of draft picks. McCabe prospered as a triggerman on the

power play who could use his big frame to impede attackers in the Leafs zone. Never hesitant to use his body, McCabe's signature defensive move was the "can opener," a move so efficient it was targeted by league officials in the crackdown on obstruction.

When asked whether making it to the NHL was a childhood dream, McCabe responded, "It's all I ever wanted to do. My parents put me on skates when I was two and by the time I was five all I was saying was I want to be an NHL player. And a funny story: I did a book report in about Grade 6 about what you want to be when you get older and I did 'a hockey player' – and the teacher wouldn't accept it because it wasn't a real job!"

DARCY TUCKER

RIGHT WING •1999–2000 TO 2007–08

Born: **March 15, 1975, Castor, Alberta**
Games: **531** Goals: **148** Assists: **171** Points: **319** PIMs: **756**

One of Darcy Tucker's greatest life lessons came on a frozen pond just behind his farm in Endiang, Alberta. He was 11 years old and playing keepaway with his little brother. His mom, Flo, was on the pond too. Darcy was having an easy time of it when Flo asked if he wanted to try it on her. Darcy tried to push the puck between his mom's skates and pick it up behind her. "Bang, forearm shiver, knocked me right on my ass," Tucker once recalled. "I looked up at my mom and said, 'What did you do that for?' 'I want you to know,' she said, 'life isn't always easy.'"

Hockey was never easy for Darcy Tucker, but he made it harder for those he was playing against. Tucker got the most of his five foot 10 and 170 pounds, but he was more than an agitator. By the end of his career, he had recorded four 20-goal seasons. The child of the prairie never forgot the tough lessons of the frozen pond.

Tucker had been inculcated for life as a Leaf long before he reached Toronto. "See that guy there?" his dad, Dale, would say when a Leafs game was carried in Alberta. "Number 17. That's a hockey player. Wendel Clark. Plays hard, plays hurt. Sticks up for his teammates."

"My dad always said: a hockey player gives his all, every night. When I play, I have my teeth gritted and my nose to the grindstone," Tucker said.

Tucker's job was to make playing the Leafs as much of an ordeal as possible.

"He sets a level of anger for everyone," his coach, Paul Maurice, once said. "You need guys like that."

For many nights over his eight years with the club, Tucker ignited his teammates and Leafs fans alike. Tucker's game burned through his small frame; he was done at 33.

"I've loved this franchise since the moment I got here," said Darcy Tucker. "There's nothing better than being a Toronto Maple Leaf. I didn't grow up watching the Leafs in Toronto, but I grew up on a farm, and when I wasn't playing hockey, I was working my ass off. I think the fans see how much I want to win, how hard I'll work to win."

Darcy Tucker taking a faceoff with Chris Herperger of the Chicago Blackhawks

ED
BELFOUR

GOALTENDER • 2002–03 TO 2005–06

Born: **April 21, 1965, Carman, Manitoba**
Games: **170** Wins: **93** Losses: **61** Ties: **15** Shutouts: **17** Goals against: **2.51**
Inducted into Hockey Hall of Fame: **2011**

E d Belfour was relentless. Relentless in his desire to be an outstanding goalie. Relentless in pursuing every edge to get there.

"I'm Ed Belfour, I'm going to be your number-one goalie," he told the Chicago Blackhawks coaching staff when he arrived.

Belfour was an undrafted player with less than two big leagues seasons of pro experience, but he was right. Belfour won a Calder as the league's top rookie in Chicago, a Stanley Cup in Dallas, and succeeded Curtis Joseph in Toronto.

He did things his way. He had a custom machine to sharpen his skates, which he brought from stop to stop. "I'd walk out of the dressing room at 1 a.m. and Eddie would still be there, working on his blades," remembered coach Pat Quinn.

"I think Eddie has a bedroom in the back of the dressing room," cracked Tie Domi.

Belfour's game day routine was precise. When he was playing on the road, he even insisted on a certain brand of orange juice. He stretched his troublesome

Ed Belfour, 2011 Hockey Hall of Fame inductee, November 14, 2011

back and corresponding muscles, studied videos, and readied himself all day long. Every detail of his equipment drew his unflagging attention. Everything was timed and executed to the minute.

"I'm very picky, especially when it comes to my professional life," Belfour once said. "Anything I care about is really precise and detailed. I want it to be perfect."

His motivation was simple enough. Overlooked by the hockey network as a kid, he was now determined to be impossible to ignore – one of the best goalies of all time. "I've always set my goals high," he once said. "I want to be part of that top group. That's where I see myself. That's what I've always tried to do."

GARY ROBERTS

LEFT WING • 2000–01 TO 2003–04

Born **May 23, 1966, North York, Ontario**
Games: **237** Goals: **83** Assists: **74** Points: **157** PIMs: **266**

Gary Roberts's story is about the victory of will. Growing up in Whitby, Ontario, Roberts was so troubled by asthma that he had to occasionally be hooked up to a machine in hospital to help him breath. As a 12-year-old, Roberts even had to give up hockey and concentrate on regaining his health. The asthma lessened as he grew into his teens but flared up again in college. Roberts's asthma would trouble him throughout his professional career.

Roberts always had a hard-driving style of attacking the net, but in the early junctures of his career, his body couldn't take the pounding. An unending series of crosschecks finally severely damaged his neck and he was forced to retire at 30.

"I thought I was done," he said. "I was in the prime of my career and all of a sudden the phone stopped ringing."

By his own admission, Roberts spent the first summer of his new life playing golf and eating chicken wings.

"That's when I realized I was not healthy for life in general," he said. "I couldn't play two golf games in a row without getting spasms in my back. I got healthy because I didn't like the way I felt or the way I looked."

But a funny thing happened as Roberts started to take care of his body. Massage therapists began making steady progress in treating his

Gary Roberts skates past Mike Keane of the St. Louis Blues

neck injury. Roberts threw himself into recovery and got his career back. But the Gary Roberts who returned to the league now had a body that could withstand his pounding style.

Gary Roberts reinvented himself as one of the most fit and powerful players in franchise history. Roberts arrived with the Leafs as a 34-year-old free agent and immediately bolstered not just the club's talent level but the commitment to the game of every player.

Roberts's competitiveness was contagious. He thrived going to the highly contested areas: the slot and the crease. "Gary has made a career," said his lifelong friend Joe Nieuwendyk, "of the three-foot goal."

"He is a guy that any team would love to have, a heart-and-soul guy," said defenceman Bryan McCabe. "Guys who make people around them better as he does are few and far between."

Roberts, whose first retirement came after 583 games, would play a total of 1,224, including 237 as a Leaf, until he retired for a final time at 42. He squeezed everything he could out of his second career.

"I was told I was never going to play again and I got a second chance," he said. "I was always grateful."

MATS SUNDIN

CENTRE • 1994–95 TO 2007–08

Born: **February 13, 1971, Bromma, Sweden**
Games: **981** Goals: **420** Assists: **567** Points: **987** PIMs: **748**
Awards: **Mark Messier Leadership Award, 2008**
Inducted into Hockey Hall of Fame: **2012**

Over 13 seasons, Mats Sundin's talent towered above the men with whom he shared the Leafs dressing room, but it was his passion and humility teammates remember most.

Never a winner of a scoring title, never a member of a team that advanced past the Stanley Cup semi-final, Mats Sundin was nevertheless the finest Maple Leaf of his era and perhaps of any era.

Sundin has a stanglehold on Leafs records. He owns the mark for most regular season goals, points, game-winning goals (79), and power-play goals (124).

Sundin garnered 70 points in 77 playoff games, a mark bettered only by Doug Gilmour and Darryl Sittler and superior to that compiled by Dave Keon, Wendel Clark, Ted Kennedy, George Armstrong, Gary Roberts, and Dave Andreychuk.

Sundin's 13 team scoring titles (12 with the Leafs) are the third most in NHL history, behind only Gordie Howe with 17 and Wayne Gretzky, who had 19. The great Darryl Sittler managed eight team scoring titles.

The dominant memory of Sundin may be his 500th NHL goal, a short-handed, overtime game-winner struck against the Calgary Flames.

Roberts had one of the best lines about playing with Sundin.

"We cycle the puck down low a lot," Roberts said. "My job is to get the puck to Mats and try not to get called for interference."

Mats Sundin faces off against the St. Louis Blues

"Year after year he was the best player on a team that was regularly fighting for the conference final," said long-time teammate Darcy Tucker. "What does that tell you?"

Pat Quinn said Sundin was the ultimate team player. "When you had a player like Mats, you could put the better players on other lines to get more balance," said Quinn. "The thing about Mats was it was never about Mats. All that mattered was that he wanted to win at the end of the night."

The fans saw a talented giant on the ice. The players saw a player of equal scale in the dressing room. "A lot of those teams had some very powerful factions," Quinn said, "and each player had his guy in the media who he would leak stuff to. It would never be Mats, but when we hit the ice there would be no division. He was the only person who all the factions could identify as being the team's true leader."

Invariably, Sundin took questions that contained the word *you* and gave answers built on the word *we*.

"Mats was always just as happy when someone else scored as when he did," said Wendel Clark. "He wanted to do well, but what he wanted more was for everyone to do well."

Sundin made his feelings about Toronto clear when he teared up after he returned to Toronto during a brief cameo with the Vancouver Canucks and scored the shootout winner.

"It was an honour for me to play in the NHL and an honour to spend all those seasons in Toronto," Sundin said. "I'll always be glad I got the chance to do it."

TIE
DOMI

RIGHT WING • 1989–90/1994–95 TO 2005–06

Born: **November 1, 1969, Windsor, Ontario**
Games: **777** Goals: **84** Assists: **112** Points: **196** PIMs: **2,265**

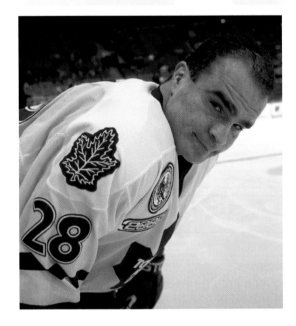

Tie Domi took part in 270 NHL fights, the vast majority while a Maple Leaf, but it is a tribute to his staying power that he was one of the rare tough guys to manage a 1,000-game career.

Like most fighters, he found anguish in the job. "Everybody in that dressing room, if there's something that has to happen, they are looking at one or two guys," Domi said. "That feeling, being the guy that has to do that, it's not an easy role ... There are nights when I've had injuries to my hand or my shoulder. The other team doesn't know that. Eighteen thousand people don't know that. Your teammates do, but there are no excuses."

Fans loved Domi's courage and style: he would consistently fight much bigger men, spinning them in circles until he could get a hand free to land a punch. Domi was immensely popular with his teammates. "He certainly looked after me and I'll owe him that for the rest of my life," said Mats Sundin.

Domi's standing as a dressing room joker, Sundin said, was central to the identity of the teams he played on. "When you play in a market like Toronto where you're under the microscope, a guy like Tie keeps things loose."

Domi understood the social element of the game. He took an interest in rookies and tutored the Leafs' apprenticing fighters.

Wendel Clark of the Chicago Blackhawks and Tie Domi

"When I got here I was a young buck and I didn't have any style as far as fighting goes," Wade Belak said upon Domi's retirement. "He showed me how to keep my balance and helped me stick around. I owe him a lot."

Domi didn't score often, he banged home 84 goals, or just under 8 a year, but he was a good skater who could take the body and take an active part in the forecheck. He potted 15 goals, a career high, in 2002–03. Off the ice, he was an unabashed media star, good with a quote, and an astute businessman. When the Leafs bought Domi out of the final year of his contract, Leafs fans said goodbye to one of their most beloved players.

15

TOMAS KABERLE

DEFENCE • 1998-99 TO 2010–11

Born: **March 2, 1978, Rakovnik, Czech Republic**
Games: **878** Goals: **83** Assists: **437** Points: **520** PIMs: **246**

Unheralded and an afterthought at the draft table, Tomas Kaberle walked right through rookie and training camp and made the Leafs as a 19-year-old in 1998.

"Not many people were planning on him being on our team, but he made it because he was a heads-up player who had the mechanics to make a good pass and the vision and intelligence to make the right pass," said Pat Quinn.

Kaberle was the embodiment of the hockey maxim that while the draft sorts out where a player starts, his play determines where he ends up. Kaberle was a Leaf two years after going 204th overall in the 1996 draft. He waited six hours before his named was called. The only defenceman drafted that year who enjoyed a better career than Kaberle was Zdeno Chara.

Kaberle, always a pass-first player, was particularly effective when paired with Bryan McCabe. More than half of McCabe's goals came on the power play and countless one-time drives were delivered thanks to Kaberle's unerring D-to-D passes.

"To me, Tommy is a big part of any success I have had," McCabe said. "I've said before I think he's the best defenceman in the NHL and I'll say it every time."

Through most of his Leafs career, Kaberle stood out as one of the best passing defenceman in the team's history. Only Borje Salming, with 620 assists, finished with more helpers than the 437 collected by the Czech defender. Kaberle is also second in the franchise for points from the blueline with 528.

The soft-spoken Kaberle would garner 984 games as an NHLer. It turns out the six-hour wait to hear his name called was well worth it.

"I've been happy here. Toronto has been my home away from home. That made it easy."

Phil Kessel, Dion Phaneuf, and Joffrey Lupul celebrate a goal by Lupul in a game against the Calgary Flames, October 15, 2011

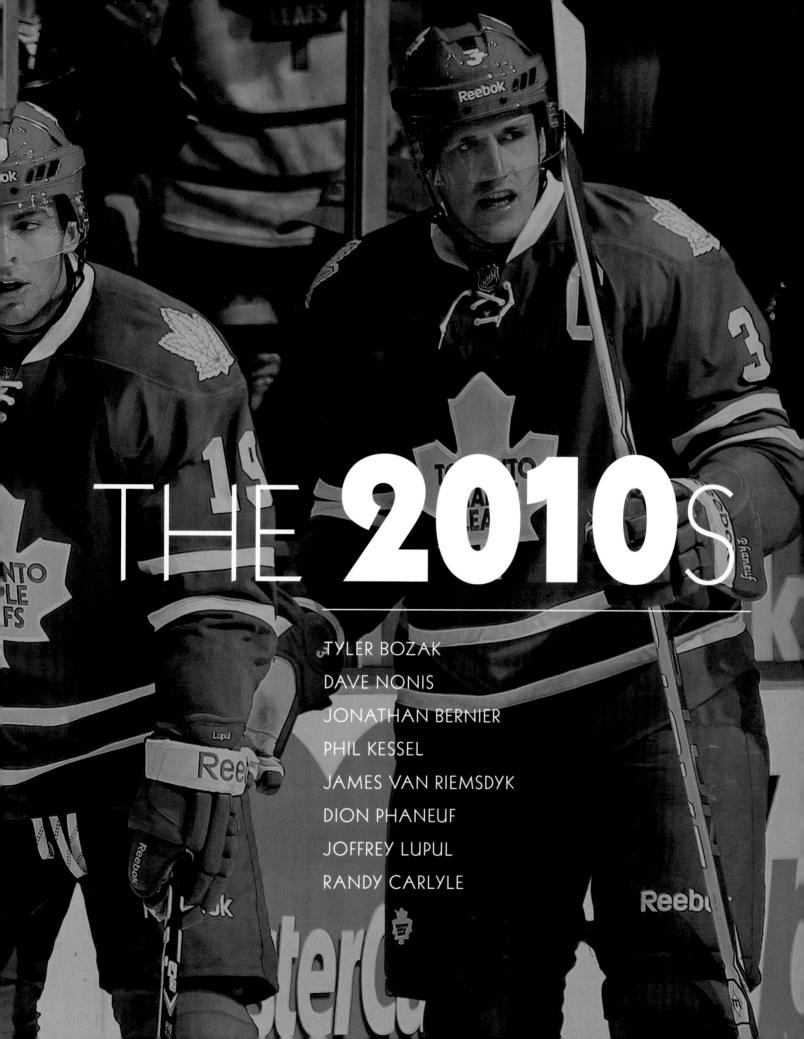

THE 2010s

TYLER BOZAK

DAVE NONIS

JONATHAN BERNIER

PHIL KESSEL

JAMES VAN RIEMSDYK

DION PHANEUF

JOFFREY LUPUL

RANDY CARLYLE

Morgan Rielly celebrates his first career NHL goal against the Pittsburgh Penguins, December 16, 2013

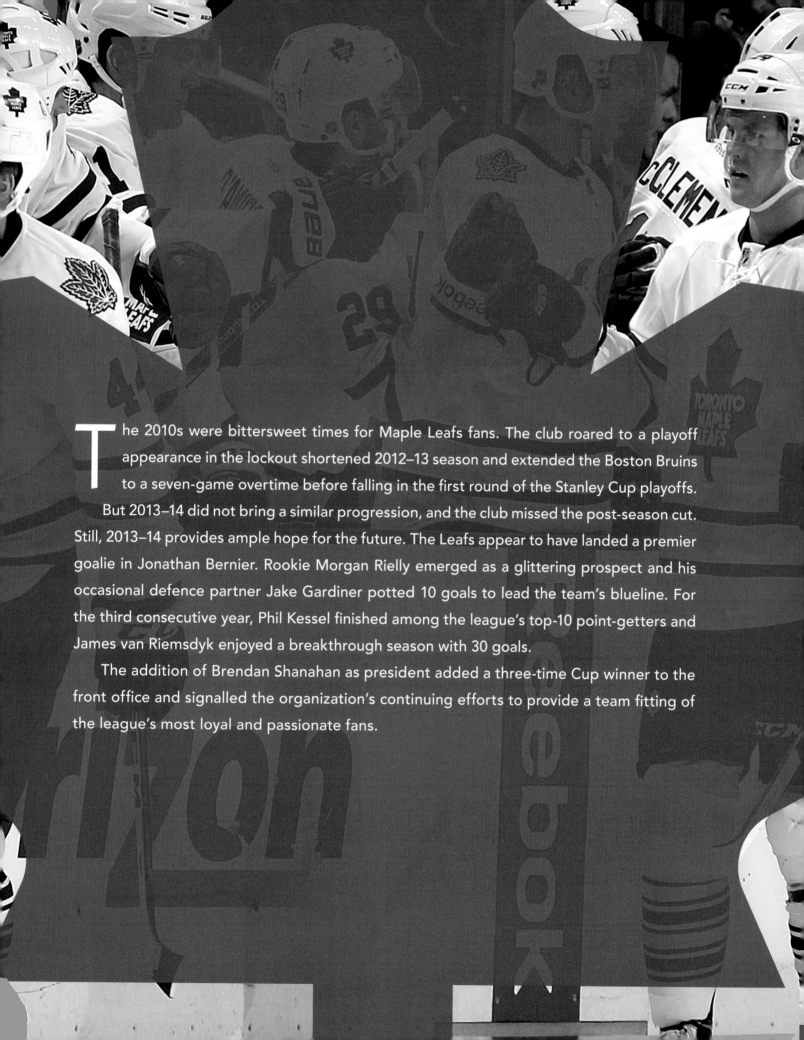

The 2010s were bittersweet times for Maple Leafs fans. The club roared to a playoff appearance in the lockout shortened 2012–13 season and extended the Boston Bruins to a seven-game overtime before falling in the first round of the Stanley Cup playoffs. But 2013–14 did not bring a similar progression, and the club missed the post-season cut. Still, 2013–14 provides ample hope for the future. The Leafs appear to have landed a premier goalie in Jonathan Bernier. Rookie Morgan Rielly emerged as a glittering prospect and his occasional defence partner Jake Gardiner potted 10 goals to lead the team's blueline. For the third consecutive year, Phil Kessel finished among the league's top-10 point-getters and James van Riemsdyk enjoyed a breakthrough season with 30 goals.

The addition of Brendan Shanahan as president added a three-time Cup winner to the front office and signalled the organization's continuing efforts to provide a team fitting of the league's most loyal and passionate fans.

Tyler Bozak and Erik Karlsson of the Ottawa Senators

TYLER BOZAK

CENTRE • 2013–14 TO PRESENT

Born: **March, 19, 1986, Regina, Saskatchewan**
Games: **296** Goals: **72** Assists: **111** Points: **183** PIMs: **62**

They were a Junior A team called the Victoria Salsa and the five-foot-nine, 18-year-old walk-on centreman was on the bubble to make the 2004–05 version of the club.

"The NHL seemed the furthest thing away my first year in Victoria," Tyler Bozak said. "I was an undersized buy. I wasn't even sure I was going to make the team and while I did I didn't play much in the first half of the year. We got a new coach and he started to play me a little bit and things turned around from there."

An undrafted free agent picked up by the Leafs after two years at the University of Denver, Bozak has emerged as a key Leaf whose heady offensive play, aptitude in the faceoff circle, and defensive excellence earned him recognition as the club's most complete forward. Bozak is the classic late bloomer. A last-minute growth spurt lifted him from five foot nine to a little under six feet, and while he lacks the frame of a dominant first-line centre Bozak's intelligent play has won legions of admirers.

"Every hockey player would like to be six foot four and 240 pounds," said Leafs' coach Randy Carlyle. "It doesn't always work out that way. Bozie has the skill set, body makeup and tools to be a real good player. We'll take the hockey sense and the hockey smarts and his prowess on the draws and offensive abilities and try to utilize him in as many situations as possible."

It might have taken him a long time to become a professional but he got to the league and the first line quickly enough. Bozak's apprenticeship with the Marlies lasted only 32 games. With Bozak the last player out of his zone and habitually unselfish with the puck, hard-skating offensive talents such as Phil Kessel and James van Riemsdyk can occasionally gamble knowing their centreman is literally and figuratively behind them.

"It's always great to play with great players, they make the game a lot easier for you," Bozak said. "You give Phil Kessel the puck and there's a good chance he's going to put it in the back of the net for you. I like to be a playmaker so it's good to play with a guy who can snipe like that."

DAVID
NONIS

GENERAL MANAGER • 2013 TO PRESENT

Born: **May 25, 1966, Burnaby, British Columbia**

September 18, 2010, Maple Leafs brass, from left: assistant VP hockey operations David Nonis, general manager Brian Burke, assistant general manager Claude Loiselle, VP hockey operations Dave Poulin, and coach Ron Wilson.

David Nonis's first public words in the press conference announcing his hiring as Leafs GM spoke volumes: "I'll be brief," he said.

Soft-spoken and a little reserved, Nonis has limited taste for publicity. "I don't think the focus should be on me," he said. "We're going to use the people we have, and I believe we have good people. It's not about one person doing the job."

He is also decisive. Fresh off a season in which the Leafs qualified for the playoffs for the first time in seven years, Nonis moved to improve the team's goaltending by trading for Jonathan Bernier, landed a proven winner in Dave Bolland, reeled in free agent David Clarkson, and gave lengthy contract extensions to key players Dion Phaneuf and Phil Kessel.

Nonis did not play in the NHL but played college hockey at the University of Maine, where he met Brian Burke, then a player agent and a future mentor. Nonis began attracting attention in the Canucks' hockey operations, negotiating contracts at just 24. At 37, he was the youngest GM in team history.

JONATHAN BERNIER

GOALTENDER • 2013 TO PRESENT

Born: **August 7, 1988, Laval, Quebec**

Games: **55** Wins: **26** Losses: **19** OTL: **7** Shutouts: **1** Goals against: **2.70**

I f you were looking for the definitive word to describe Leafs goalie Jonathan Bernier, *calm* would be a great place to start.

"I'm a pretty casual guy," Bernier said. "I don't get stressed about too much."

Bernier projects that relaxed air on the ice. The greater the action around the crease, the more settled Bernier seems.

"He's so calm in there and so confident," said Joffrey Lupul. "He controls rebounds and controls the puck certainly unlike any goalie I've ever played with."

The path to the Leafs net was far from easy. Drafted 11th overall in 2006, Bernier did not become an NHL regular until he was 25 and traded by the team that drafted him, the Los Angeles Kings, to Toronto. Bernier said that despite 152 games in the American League and four years in Los Angeles backing up Jonathan Quick, he wouldn't change a thing.

"I'm not the type of person who wants to change things from the past. You have to move forward. I believe

if you go through some down time or when negative things happen that's a good thing. You need negative things sometimes as incentive to do better."

Bernier watched from the bench as Quick captured the Conn Smythe Trophy as best playoff performer in the Kings' 2012 Stanley Cup run.

"Winning the Cup was a great moment for me, even if I didn't play, but playing a lot is really satisfying," he said. "I love being around my teammates and I love to compete. To get the chance to do that in Toronto has been great."

PHIL KESSEL

81

RIGHT WING • 2013 TO PRESENT

Born: **October 2, 1987, Madison, Wisconsin**
Games: **364** Goals: **156** Assists: **177** Points: **333** PIMs: **110**
Awards: **Bill Masterton Trophy, 2007**

Phil Kessel is excitement. The Leafs' most consistent breakaway threat is a natural, a phenomenal skater with an unerring sense of where the puck is going. Kessel scores goals in bunches thanks to a tremendous snapshot and a constant determination to go to the net. He also flashes elite passing skills.

Kessel was born to the role of athletic superstar. His father, Phil Sr., was a collegiate quarterback drafted by the Washington Redskins. The New York Islanders drafted his brother, Blake, and his sister, Amanda, like her brother, was an NCAA star who shone in the United States Olympic Program.

Leafs general manager Brian Burke acquired Kessel, the fifth overall pick in 2006, for two first-round draft choices and a second in a deal that was widely panned and then grudgingly admired.

From the beginning, Kessel gave the Leafs the game-breaking talent they had long needed. Kessel would register 20-, 32-, and 37-goal seasons for the Leafs in his first three seasons in Toronto. Along the way, Kessel has learned to develop a better all-around

Phil Kessel walks out to the ice on a night that ends in a Leafs overtime win against the Edmonton Oilers, October 12, 2013

game in keeping with the demands of coach Randy Carlyle.

"The idea out there was we wouldn't get along," Carlyle said. "That's totally unfair. I don't expect Phil to be the team's best defensive player, that's not his game. My expectations for Phil were that he had to play more stop-and-go [defence] and I think he does that."

A quiet person who prefers life outside the spotlight, Kessel inked an eight-year contract extension in 2013. He will score plenty of goals and have very little to say about it.

"I know he's quiet with the media but I'm really impressed with Phil as a teammate," said David Clarkson.

"I know he's shy outside the room," said defenceman Carl Gunnarsson, "but inside, he's a great team guy."

James van Riemsdyk celebrates his goal against
the Philadelphia Flyers. The Leafs won 5–2

JAMES VAN RIEMSDYK

LEFT WING • 2012–13 TO PRESENT

Born: **May 4, 1989, Middletown, New Jersey**
Games: **128** Goals: **48** Assists: **45** Points: **93** PIMs: **76**

It was a slogan printed out and stuck on the wall of James van Riemsdyk's bedroom in Middletown, New Jersey. "I think my dad put it up when I was in middle school and I've always believed it," van Riemsdyk said. "If you fail to prepare, you prepare for failure."

Van Riemsdyk, a highly touted product of the U.S. development system, endured uneven results early in his NHL career. A constant eye toward preparation and maximizing his abundant physical skills has made him an impact player with the Maple Leafs.

Six foot three and gifted with tremendous skating skills and hands for a big man, van Riemsdyk was chosen second overall by the Philadelphia Flyers in the 2007 entry draft. Van Riemsdyk delivered 15-, 21-, and 11-goal seasons for the Flyers, but a procession of injuries seemed to negate his promise in Philadelphia. Traded for defenceman Luke Schenn, van Riemsdyk enjoyed immediate chemistry with fleet winger Phil Kessel and centre Tyler Bozak by going to the net.

"He's not afraid to go to the dirty areas at all," said Bozak. "He battles the biggest guys out there, and he's gotten better and better at it because he works extremely hard on and off the ice."

Loyalty, to teammates and family, is at the centre of his values. When he was 15 and playing in high school for the Christian Brothers Academy in New Jersey, van Riemsdyk was recruited to try out for the national program. The tryout would have conflicted with the school's playoff. Van Riemsdyk told USA Hockey they would have to wait and ended up scoring the winning goal in the state championship.

"I'm happy I made the commitment to stay loyal to my team," he said. "It's something we will remember for the rest of our lives. Those people, friends, family, teammates, they are most important to me. That comes first for me: maintaining those relationships and being there for the people who are important in my life."

DION
PHANEUF

C DEFENCE • 2010–11 TO PRESENT

Born: **April 10, 1985, Edmonton, Alberta**
Games: **302** Goals: **39** Assists: **104** Points: **143** PIMs: **423**

3

Dion Phaneuf watches from the bench during a game
against the Nashville Predators, October 10, 2013

Since June 14, 2010, the Maple Leafs have belonged to captain Dion Phaneuf. The team bestowed the C in a ceremony attended by former captains Darryl Sittler, George Armstrong, and Wendel Clark. Phaneuf, the team's 19th captain, accepted the letter as a token of his willingness to be the Leafs' hardest worker.

He learned leadership from watching former Flames captain Jarome Iginla and said he would model his demeanour on leaders such as Mark Messier, Scott Stevens, and Clark.

"You look at how they play the game and how they lead," Phaneuf said. "I think the best way to lead is you don't have to be the loudest guy, but you definitely want to be the guy who's working the hardest day in and day out."

From the first, Phaneuf has been the Leafs' leader in ice time among defencemen. A one-time 20-goal scorer, Phaneuf quieted his game to maximize his time on the ice.

Phaneuf welcomed wearing the C in the hothouse that is Toronto.

"I'm very comfortable being in this role," he said. "Obviously when you go through tough times — whether as an individual player or as a team — people will be critical. I understand that. But you learn a lot when you go through those tough times, the times that aren't fun, as a team and as an organization. In a city like Toronto, there's lots of criticism. I'll do everything I can to help this team win."

JOFFREY LUPUL

19

RIGHT WING, LEFT WING • 2010–11 TO PRESENT

Born: **September 23, 1983, Fort Saskatchewan, Alberta**
Games: **179** Goals: **67** Assists: **80** Points: **147** PIMs: **123**

Joffrey Lupul is a man in the moment. He travels extensively in the off-season and reviews musical acts for online magazines. He has been featured in *ESPN: The Body Issue*. Model, music critic, world traveller, Lupul has managed a handful of interests while keeping his day job as a hockey player.

That part, the athlete part, was at one time in doubt.

In 2009, Lupul underwent back surgery for a herniated disk. The operation didn't take and another was performed, but during follow-up testing, a potentially lethal blood infection was found. Lupul spent two months in bed, with friends and family helping to administer an IV. In the end, he missed 12 months and many doubted he could resume his career.

"I figured I'd play until I was 35 and everything would go smooth," Lupul said. "Then something like this happens, and you see how close you can be to your career being over. I have a greater appreciation for how lucky we are to play in the NHL."

When he arrived in Toronto in a February 2011 trade, Lupul re-dedicated himself to being a pro. Now one of the best-conditioned Leafs, Lupul's top-drawer offensive skills have made him a potent force.

Lupul remains, when healthy, an excellent offensive player. He has scored 25 or more goals three times in his NHL career, and he approaches the net fearlessly.

"He just plays the game at a higher level and works at a higher level than a lot of people," Leafs coach Randy Carlyle said. "That's a great example for our younger players."

23

RANDY CARLYLE

DEFENCE • 1976–77 TO 1977–78
COACH • 2013–14 TO PRESENT

Born: **April 19, 1956, Sudbury, Ontario**
Games (player): **94** Goals: **2** Assists: **16** Points: **18** PIMs: **82**
Games (coach): **148** Record: **70 W, 62 L, 16 OTL** Pts. %: **.527**

Randy Carlyle, 2014

While he played only 94 games for the Leafs, Randy Carlyle's story has a blue-and-white background. First, like so many key figures in Maple Leaf history – Frank Mahovlich, Dave Keon, George Armstrong – Carlyle came to Toronto from northern Ontario. Second, as a Leafs rookie in 1976, he played for Red Kelly, one of the linchpins of the 1967 Stanley Cup champions. Third, he played with three Hall of Fame Leafs in Toronto: Lanny McDonald, Darryl Sittler, and Borje Salming. And finally, like Hap Day, Joe Primeau, King Clancy, Howie Meeker, Kelly, George Armstrong, Pat Quinn, Ron Wilson, and a handful of others, Carlyle is coaching the franchise he played for.

"For a kid from Ontario to get a second opportunity to represent the Toronto Maple Leafs, well I feel very fortunate," Carlyle said upon his hiring.

A Norris Trophy winner and Stanley Cup–winning coach with the Anaheim Ducks, Carlyle blends old school with new. There is little question about who is boss.

"Randy," said Hall of Famer Scott Bowman, an expert on these matters, "keeps his players accountable."

Carlyle teams are in shape, defensively oriented, and defined by values as old as the game itself. "Every successful team has stressed defence," Carlyle said. "There's nothing new in that. The next game is always the most important game of the season. It's not about next week, it's about tonight,

Randy Carlyle during a game against
the St. Louis Blues, November 6, 1976

Randy Carlyle during a break in play in a game against the Winnipeg Jets, February 7, 2013

the first shift, the first period, being first on the puck, getting the first bodycheck, drawing the first penalty, scoring first. That's how you play the game."

And yet, there is in Carlyle an acknowledgement that the game is played by human beings with emotions that need to be tended. In his first press conference as a Leafs coach, Carlyle said his job was to "rekindle the spirit" of a downtrodden team and to "help the players feel good about themselves."

Drafted 30th overall by the Leafs in 1976, Carlyle racked up 1,055 NHL games. After Toronto, he starred in Pittsburgh where he won a Norris Trophy in 1981, and Winnipeg. More success came when he moved behind the bench. Carlyle spent six seasons as coach of the Manitoba Moose, two years as an assistant with the Washington Capitals, and then returned to the Moose.

Carlyle was an instant success when he returned to the NHL. The Ducks made the conference final in his first campaign and won the Cup in 2007. He has never endured a losing season in a full NHL campaign.

In Carlyle's first season, he returned the Leafs to the playoffs and extended the Boston Bruins to overtime in the seventh game of their opening round. A late-season swoon knocked the Leafs out of the post-season in 2013–14.

The Leafs gave Carlyle a two-year contract extension in 2014. General Manager Dave Nonis said Carlyle was the right man despite the team's disappointing season.

"In Randy, we know that we have a leader who has enjoyed a high level of success as both a player and a coach, including a Stanley Cup championship," Nonis said.

Exclusivity, the idea that playing professional hockey is a privilege to be cherished by the lucky few is at the centre of Carlyle's value system.

"That's how you create unity within your group," Carlyle said. "That all for one, one for all mentality is what successful teams and successful organizations have to be able to do. . . . The name on the front of the sweater is more important than the name on the back."

Somewhere, Conn Smythe was smiling.

From left: Bill Ezinicki, Coach Hap Day, Ted Kennedy, and Gus Mortson, April 12, 1949. Day had promised to wear the hat he had received as a gift if the team won three straight games

PHOTO CREDITS

HOCKY HALL OF FAME:

Copyright Page (Graphic Artists); Introduction (Hockey Hall of Fame); 2-3 (Imperial Oil-Turofsky); 4-5 (Hockey Hall of Fame); 6 (Imperial Oil-Turofsky); 9-15 (Imperial Oil-Turofsky); 16 (Le Studio du Hockey); 18 (Imperial Oil-Turofsky); 20-23 (Imperial Oil-Turofsky); 24 (Le Studio du Hockey); 25-61(Imperial Oil-Turofsky); 62 (Michael Burns Sr.); 63-64 (Imperial Oil-Turofsky); 65 (Frank Prazak); 66-78 (Imperial Oil-Turofsky); 79-83 (Graphic Artists); 84-85 (Imperial Oil-Turofsky); 86 (Graphic Artists); 87-89 (Imperial Oil-Turofsky); 90 (Hockey Hall of Fame); 91-96 (Imperial Oil-Turofsky); 97 (Graphic Artists); 98-99 (Imperial Oil-Turofsky); 100-101, 103 (Graphic Artists); 104 (O-Pee-Chee Collection); 105-107 (Frank Prazak); 110-111, 113 (Bob Shaver); 114 (Graphic Artists); 115-116 (Portnoy); 117, 120-121 (Graphic Artists); 122 (Frank Prazak); 125 (Portnoy); 126-130 (Graphic Artists); 131-132 (Portnoy); 133 (Graphic Artists); 135 (Bob Shaver); 136 (Graphic Artists); 137 (Mecca); 138 (Portnoy); 139 (Graphic Artists); 141 (Steve Poirier); 142-143 (Portnoy); 144-145, 147 (Bob Shaver); 148 (O-Pee-Chee); 149-150 (Paul Bereswill); 151(Graphic Artists); 152-153 (Portnoy); 154 (Miles Nadal); 155 (Graphic Artists); 156 (O-Pee-Chee); 157 (Mecca); 158 (Portnoy); 159-160 (Paul Bereswill); 161-162 (Doug MacLellan); 163-165 (Dave Sandford); 168-170 (Doug MacLellan); 171 (Dave Sandford); 173 (Paul Bereswill); 174-177 [top] (Doug MacLellan); 177 [bottom] (Chris Relke); 178, 181-183 (Doug MacLellan); 184-189, 191-192 (Dave Sandford); 193-194 (Doug MacLellan); 195 (Graphic Artists); 196-197, 200 (Dave Sandford); 201 (Graphic Artists); 202-205, 207-208 (Dave Sanford); 209 (Matthew Manor); 210-212 (Dave Sandford); 213 (Matthew Manor); 214-217, 219, 224, 227-228, 230, 235, 237 (Dave Sandford); 239 (Portnoy); 242, 244-245 (Imperial Oil-Turofksy); 246 (Graphic Artists)

GETTY IMAGES:

7 (B Bennett); 8 (Yale Joel); 112 (Denis Brodeur); 119, 123, 124 (Steve Babineau); 190 (Graig Abel); 222 (Gregory Shamus); 226 (Andrew Francis Wallace); 229 (Steve Russell); 232 (Rene Johnston); 234 (Frederick Breedon); 238 (Graig Abel); 240 (Marianne Helm)

TEAM PHOTOS:

144-45 courtesy Dennis Miles; 166-67 and 198-99 courtesy Graig Abel

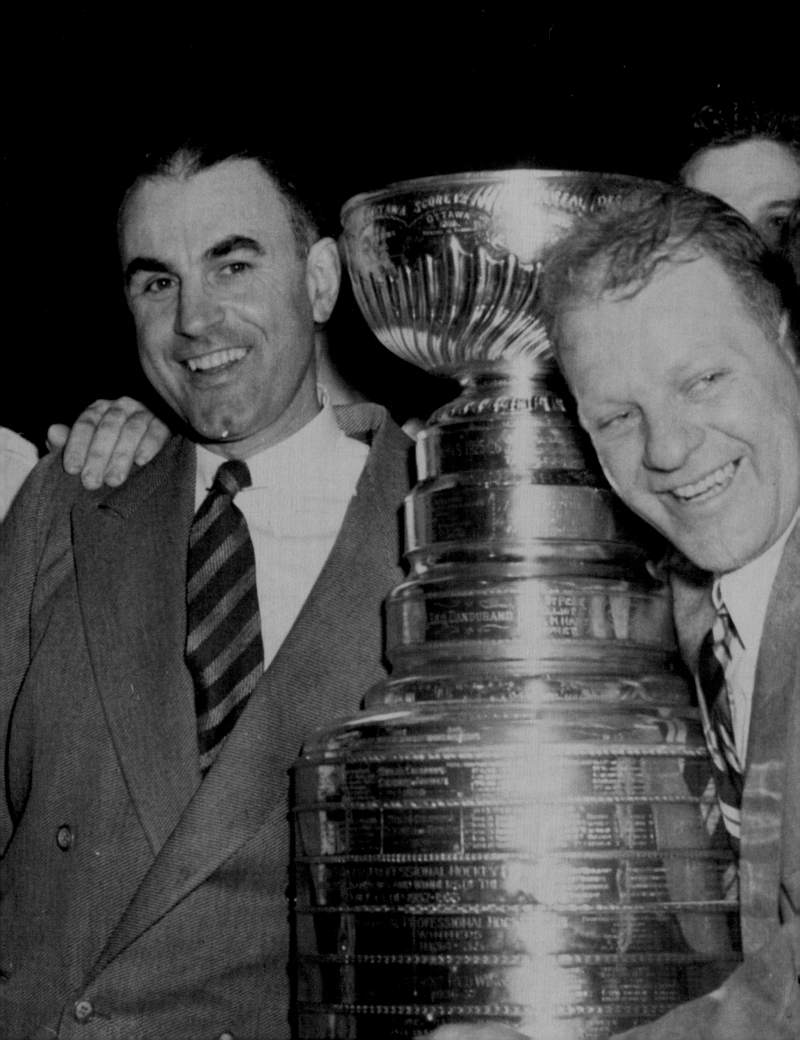

Captain George Armstrong (left) and Frank Mahovlich
celebrate their Stanley Cup win, April 18, 1963

INDEX